AROUND CARDIFF
BY TROLLEYBUS

This book is dedicated to the memory of
Doctor Colin Hewlett 1944 - 2020
A Dear Friend and fellow trolleybus enthusiast

By Peter Smith

Published by Adam Gordon

BUT/East Lancs 221 passes one of Cardiff's main tourest attractions, Cardiff Castle, as it makes it way along Castle Street towards The Royal Oak in the summer of 1964. The Castle was built in the 19th Century (on the site of a Roman Fort dating back over 2,000 years) by the 3rd Marquess of Bute using his vast wealth to finance the project. The architect was William Burges. *John White*

Front Cover: BUT/Bruce Coachworks 271 negotiates the turning circle at the Roath Park terminus of Service 3 in early April 1968. *M.J. Russell*

Rear Cover: BUT/East Lancs 280 has climbed the long-drawn-out hill in Grand Avenue on October 6th 1968. 280 will now make its way to the MacDonald Road terminus of Service 10A (about half-a-mile distant). *John White*

ISBN 978-1-910654-51-4

Publication no.142

Published in 2023 by   Adam Gordon, Kintradwell Farmhouse, Brora, Sutherland, KW9 6LU
Tel: 01408 622660   E-mail: adam@ahg-books.com

Designed and typeset by   Barnabas Gordon
Tel: 07795 201 502   Email: Barney@ahg-books.com

Printed by   Henry Ling Ltd., The Dorset Press, Dorchester, DT1 1HD

ACKNOWLEDGEMENTS

I am very much indebted to my friend (and fellow Cardiff trolleybus enthusiast) John White, for his help, encouragement, and assistance in the preparation of this book. I would also like to put on record my sincere appreciation to John for allowing so many of his photographs to be depicted in this book. I have also used many photographs taken by the late Dr.Colin Hewlett, to whom this book is dedicated.

I also offer my grateful thanks to the following for allowing me to include their photographs in this book; they are in alphabetical order: Tony Belton, C. Carter, Derek Chaplin (courtesy Peter Brabham), David Christie, Malcolm Gylee, David Pearson, Robin Helliar-Symons, Carl Isgar, Robert Morris (National Tramway Museum for the use of photographs taken by H.B. Priestley), R.F. Mack (courtesy NTA 1963), R. Rowe, M.J. Russell, Hugh Taylor, D.A. Thompson, John Wiltshire (courtesy Andrew Wiltshire).

My sincere thanks also to Tudor Thomas for his excellent wiring maps.

I would also like to thank the Cardiff and South Wales Trolleybus Project (CSWTP) for their help with photographs from the R.W.A. Jones collection. My thanks also to the Cardiff Transport Preservation Group (CTPG) for their help with photographs from the late Chris Taylor collection. Also, my thanks to my partner Janet for her help and guidance and to Adam Gordon and his son Barnabas for publishing this book.

The research and preparation for this book has been an interesting and enjoyable experience for the author, and it is very much hoped that this will also be the case for the reader.

Peter Smith,
Cardiff, June 2023

BUT/East Lancs 238 has arrived at the Pier Head (Bute Street) reversing point on 2nd August 1957. The conductor has alighted and will supervise the traffic during the reversing procedure. *I.W. Wright courtesy Stephen Rowson*

INTRODUCTION

After several years of indecision, Cardiff City Council at a special Meeting held on May 8th 1939 voted in favour to implement a policy of replacing the trams by trolleybuses. The decision in favour of trolleybuses had been based mainly on a Report submitted by the City Treasurer, which not only outlined the financial benefits of operating trolleybuses, but also that if trolleybuses replaced the trams, six extra men would be required to mine the additional coal needed for their operation.

Ambitious plans to convert not only the remaining tram routes, but also the majority of the oil-bus services within the city boundary were made official policy. Due to the outbreak of war, it was not until 1st March 1942 that the first trolleybus service (between Wood Street and Clarence Road) commenced operation. A Pay-As-You-Enter system, with a flat fare of 1d was also introduced at the same time (more information about PAYE can be found in 'Route 6'). Wartime conditions prevented the acquisition of additional trolleybus chassis, and the conversion programme did not proceed any further until after hostilities had ceased.

The substitution by trolleybuses for tramcars was finally completed in February 1950, and within weeks of the last tram operating, some members of the Transport Committee were demanding that the trolleybus system should also be scrapped. However, all was not bleak and in 1953 the City Council voted in favour of the substitution by trolleybuses for oil-buses on certain services to the vast Ely housing estate, situated in the west of the city. The decision to extend to Ely was largely based on the fact that the Transport Committee had twenty-five new trolleybus chassis surplus to their requirements, and did not know what to do with them! The new trolleybus service to Ely commenced on 8th May 1955.

Following the replacement of the PAYE flat fare system by a variable fare structure in October 1950, a major reorganisation of trolleybus services commenced in October 1951 with the introduction of three new cross-town services (4, 8 and 9). These new services substantially improved travel across the city, whereas previously passengers travelling north to south or east to west had to break their journey in the central area.

Although profitable, the fate of the Cardiff trolleybus system was finally sealed in a disastrous dewirement that occurred in Castle Street on October 27th 1960. This dewirement brought down a considerable amount of overhead equipment, paralysing the whole of the city centre during the morning peak period and for several hours afterwards. In the local elections held the following May, Labour (who originally had proposed the introduction of trolleybuses in 1939 and now also supported their retention) lost control of the City Council to the Conservatives, who immediately implemented plans to scrap the trolleybus system.

Gradually the trolleybuses were replaced by oil-buses, and by late 1969 only the two Ely services were left in operation. A dispute involving craftsmen at Roath Depot brought these two services to a sudden end on 3rd December 1969. A series of special events to commemorate the closure of the system was held the following month; the final day of operation was 11th January 1970.

Peter Smith,
Cardiff, June 2023

AEC/Northern Counties 202 is seen on March 3rd 1962 in Newport Road (St. James Arcade), as it travels from Roath Depot to Castle Street to take up duties on Service 5B. In April 1954 the front of 202 was extensively damaged after it collided with a traction post in Cowbridge Road East. During the subsequent repair process, the front destination box was rebuilt similar to that found on the BUT trolleybuses. The original 'Saunders' type of headlights were also replaced by flush mounted headlights similar to those fitted to the BUT vehicles.
John White

CONTENTS

BUT/Bruce Coachworks 258 passes Woolworth's store in Albany Road, Roath, working a Service 3 journey to Roath Park on September 13th 1967. This was a busy suburban shopping area, occupied by many small (slightly up-market) businesses. The 'J. Taylor Ltd' offside advertisement was unique to 258.

John White

SERVICE 1
ST MARY STREET - GABALFA

Outward via St. Mary Street - High Street - Duke Street - Queen Street - Newport Road - City Road - Crwys Road - Whitchurch Road (Gabalfa). Inward via reverse of above route to Queen Street, then via Queen Street - St. John Street - Working Street - The Hayes - Mill Lane - St. Mary Street.

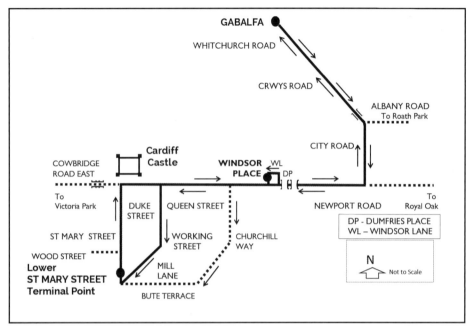

Trolleybus Service 1 commenced Monday 20th February 1950, replacing tram Service 1A and 1B.

Passing through the inner-city areas of Cathays and Roath, Service 1 connected the city centre with Gabalfa (a suburb in north east Cardiff). A wide variety of shops and terraced houses lined almost the entire length of the route. In the last few years of operation, trolleybuses interworked on Services 1 and 3 during the evening period.

The last day of trolleybus operation was Saturday 27th April 1968. Motor buses, operating over the same route, but on a reduced frequency taking over the following day. The length of the route was 3.11 miles.

The city centre terminus of Service 1 was in St. Mary Street and was shared with trolleybus Services 2 and 3. An overhead passing loop allowed trolleybuses working these routes to easily overtake one another, and BUT/East Lancs (Bridlington) 249 is seen taking advantage of this facility to overtake BUT/East Lancs 275 on 5th April 1968.   *John White*

BUT/East Lancs 220 loads at the stop outside Lloyds Bank in Queen Street on its way to Gabalfa, in the summer of 1965. The Castle Clock Tower and the former British Home Stores building can be seen in the background. Queen Street is now pedestrianised.
Colin Hewlett

Working an inward journey in 1966, BUT/East Lancs 213 is in Queen Street at its junction with Churchill Way. For a short time after conversion from tram to trolleybus operation in 1949/50, trolleybuses on Services 1, 2 and 3 travelled inward from this point via Churchill Way to reach their terminal point in St. Mary Street. This did not prove popular with passengers, and from January 13th 1951 the inward route changed to St. John Street, Working Street, The Hayes and Mill Lane.
Author's Collection

Passing beneath the former Rhymney Railway Bridge in Newport Road, is BUT/East Lancs 230 on an inward journey from Gabalfa on 11th April 1966. Going in the opposite direction on Service 4 to Roath Park is BUT/Bruce Coachworks 252.

C. Isgar

BUT/East Lancs 219 has dewired just prior to passing under a trailing frog on an inward journey from Gabalfa at the junction of City Road and Newport Road on 9th September 1966.

John White

After finishing duty on Service 1, BUT/East Lancs 276 is turning left from City Road into Newport Road to return to Roath Depot, on 23rd April 1968. The conductor can be seen pulling the handle attached to the traction post, to operate the hand-frog.

John White

9

BUT/Bruce Coachworks 251 is seen travelling south along City Road, Roath, on an inward Service 1 journey on March 19th 1967. There were many car showrooms to be found in City Road at this time. The showrooms have long since disappeared, replaced in the main by fast food shops.

John White

A busy scene at the northern end of City Road, Roath, where BUT/East Lancs 281 has just passed through the power frog on 24th April 1968. It has taken the inner set of wires to enable it to proceed in the direction of Gabalfa, whilst 218, following close behind on Service 3, will take the outer set of wires to turn right into Albany Road to continue to Roath Park.

John White

Facing in the opposite direction to the previous photograph, BUT/East Lancs 221 is about to enter City Road from Crwys Road on an inward journey from Gabalfa on February 4th 1967. Bruce Coachworks bodied AEC Regent III No. 12 waits for the green light at the junction of Mackintosh Place and Albany Road prior to turning right into Richmond Road. *John White*

BUT/East Lancs 228 crosses the bridge in Crwys Road over the Cardiff (Queen St) – Rhymney railway line on its way to Gabalfa, on September 9th 1967.

John White

A rear view of BUT/East Lancs 223 in Crwys Road, Cathays, outward to Gabalfa on 2nd February 1968. On the left, just ahead of 223 can be seen the bulbous turrets of Cathays Methodist Church, built in 1890 and still open today, although the turrets have now been removed. A Dodge lorry, going in the opposite direction, is just about to pass 223.

R. Helliar-Symons

BUT/East Lancs 223 works its way along Crwys Road, Cathays, passing a variety of local shops on its way to Gabalfa in March 1968. In a few weeks' time 223 will be withdrawn after nearly twenty years of service. The coach-built pram in the foreground is something of a rarity today.

John White

Passing along Crwys Road, Cathays and heading for the city centre in March 1968, is BUT/East Lancs 216. The Crwys Hotel on the corner of Woodville Road has in recent years undergone several face-lifts and is still open. Cathays has changed considerably since trolleybus days, and housing in this area is now largely student accommodation.

John White

BUT/East Lancs 275 approaches a power feeder in Crwys Road on 10th May 1967. In pre-motorway days this road was extremely busy, and served as the main by-pass route around Cardiff. The location has changed little over the years   *R.W.A. Jones Courtesy CSWTP*

Passing the Grade II Listed Cathays Library, BUT/East Lancs 215 is seen leaving Whitchurch Road and entering Crwys Road, on a city-bound journey from Gabalfa on 22nd January 1967. The library was built in 1907 with funding provided by the American businessman Andrew Carnegie.   *R.W.A. Jones Courtesy SWTP*

Brush car No.2 is viewed passing the Heath Hotel public house on 14th April 1939. The hotel opened in 1895, and was owned by Brains Brewery until 2020, when it was taken over by Marstons Brewery. The last remaining tram route (Service 1A/B St. Mary Street – Whitchurch Road) was converted to trolleybuses on February 20th 1950.   *H.B. Priestley*

An interesting comparison with the previous photograph. BUT/East Lancs 282 is seen at the junction of Whitchurch Road with Allensbank Road on 19th February 1966, on its way to the city centre.
John White

AEC/Northern Counties 203 stands at the original Gabalfa terminus in 1960. The building of a fly-over and underpass in the late 1960's has completely transformed this scene and nothing remains to identify its location.
John White

Trolleybuses working Services 1 and 9 turned anti-clockwise into the original Gabalfa terminus situated at the junction of Whitchurch Road/North Road/Western Avenue, where BUT/East Lancs 229 is shown operating on a short-working to Windsor Place in 1960. A new turning arrangement which avoided trolleybuses crossing the busy A470 North Road junction, was brought into use on 6th May 1961.
John White

Both photographs on this page were taken on Sunday morning 7th May 1961, when the Gabalfa turning point and terminus was relocated. Above: Commer tower wagon No. 3 is involved in cutting the trolley wire down at the former Gabalfa terminus. Below: Linesmen on tower wagon No. 2 are busy erecting trolley wire at the new terminus about 100 yards south of the old location. By lunchtime the wiring at the new turning facility was completed and in use. The first trolleybus to use the new wiring was 273. *John White*

Shown turning from Whitchurch Road into the 'Trolleybuses Only' private road, where the new Gabalfa terminus was located, are BUT/East Lancs 216 and 277 in August 1967. Two houses were compulsory purchased and demolished in connection with its construction. *John White*

Standing at the Gabalfa Terminus awaiting its return trip back to the city centre, is BUT/Bruce Coachworks 264 in June 1965. First departure on Weekdays and Saturdays from Gabalfa (1955 Timetable) was 5:22am., thereafter a 10/12-minute frequency operated throughout the day until 10:45pm. *R. Rowe*

BUT/East Lancs 279 is seen leaving the Gabalfa terminus after an unusually late fall of snow on 14th April 1966. It will shortly turn left into Whitchurch Road on its return journey to the city centre. The early 1950's Vauxhall car, seen on the right, adds interest to the photograph.　　　　　　　　　　　　　　　　　　　　　　　　　　　　*John White*

Inward trolleybuses on Services 1, 2 and 3, upon reaching the junction of Queen Street and St. John Street, turned left into St. John Street, and then travelled via Working Street, The Hayes, Mill Lane to their city centre terminal point in St. Mary Street. In this view taken on 2nd February 1966, BUT/East Lancs 219 is about to turn left from Queen Street into St. John Street.　　　　　　　　　　　　　　　　　　　　　　　　　　　　*John White*

BUT/East Lancs 217 is seen passing through The Hayes on March 30th 1968. The properties on the right at this point have since been redeveloped, but the building in the background with arched windows remains.

John White

AEC/Northern Counties 203 makes its way along Mill Lane in March 1962 The single-deck trolleybuses operating on route 14 used the inner set of wires.

John White

BUT/Bruce Coachworks 273 is seen in Mill Lane approaching the Monument Roundabout prior to reaching the terminus of Service 1 in St. Mary Street in June 1967. By this time the overhead wiring previously used by the single-deck trolleybuses had been removed.
M.J. Russell

After negotiating the Monument Roundabout, BUT/East Lancs 227 approaches the Gabalfa terminal point in St. Mary Street in June 1967.
M.J. Russell

SERVICE 2
ST. MARY STREET - PENGAM

Outward via St. Mary Street - High Street - Duke Street - Queen Street - Newport Road - Pengam Road - Clydesmuir Road. Inward was by reverse of above route to Queen Street, then via Queen Street - St. John Street - Working Street - The Hayes - Mill Lane - St. Mary Street.

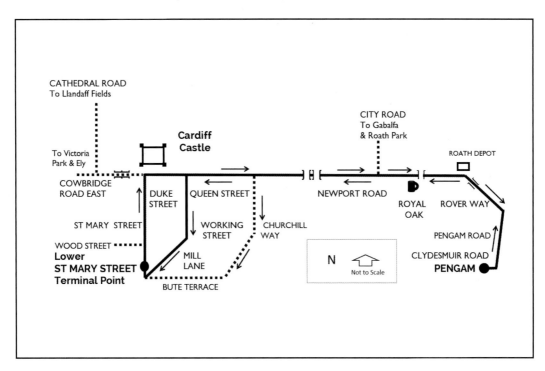

Trolleybus Service 2 commenced Sunday 15th October 1950, replacing tram routes 2A and 2B. The length of the route was 2.50 miles. Pengam is a district situated on the eastern side of Cardiff, comprising mainly council housing built in the 1930's. Service 2 passed Roath Trolleybus Depot, which was situated about half mile distant from the Pengam terminus. Following the closure of the Pengam route the wiring from the Royal Oak terminus had to be retained for accessing the Depot.

The last day of trolleybus operation was Saturday 24th November 1962. Oil-buses, operating over the same route but on a reduced frequency, taking over the following day. It was the first Cardiff trolleybus route to be abandoned after the decision had been taken to replace trolleybuses by oil-buses.

BUT/Bruce 273 is seen waiting to depart from the St. Mary Street terminus of Service 2 in 1959.
R.F. Mack, courtesy NTA 1963

Northern Counties/AEC 664T 206 has just left the terminal point of Service 2, and is seen at the junction of St. Mary Street and Wood Street during the summer of 1960. The overhead passing loop at the terminus can be seen to the rear of 206. The Pearl Insurance paper advert is typical of the period. *D.A.Thompson*

On an outward Service 2 to Pengam, BUT/Bruce Coachworks 253 waits at the traffic lights in High Street, before turning right into Duke Street on November 15th 1962. This was a very busy junction, and the overhead wiring was the most intensively used section on the system. *Tony Belton*

A general view taken from the parapet wall of Cardiff Castle showing High Street, Castle Street and Duke Street junction in 1956. An unidentified Bruce bodied trolleybus on Service 2 has just turned into Duke Street from High Street, whilst BUT/East Lancs 224 is returning to Newport Road (Roath Depot). The oil-bus (on the left) is 196, an AEC Regent with East Lancs bodywork dating from 1940.   *Author's Collection*

BUT/Bruce 256 is seen working an inward journey in Queen Street circa 1953. It has just operated the frog to allow it to turn left into St. John Street. Throughout its working life, 256 carried an offside advert for local firm Chivers.
Author's Collection

BUT/Bruce Coachworks 253 is just about to leave Newport Road and enter Pengam Road on 15th November 1962. The road alterations in the background were the main reason for the abandonment of the route (the cost of realigning the overhead and repositioning of traction posts was considered prohibitive). *Tony Belton*

Northern Counties bodied AEC 664T 201 is on its way to Pengam, and is crossing the bridge spanning the railway line from Cardiff to London. It is passing a 1958 BMC van delivering Nestles products. Period advertisements for Bristol cigarettes and Courage beers appear on hoardings in the background. *A. Wiltshire*

BUT/East Lancs 284 is seen turning from Pengam Road into Clydesmuir Road, and arriving at the discharge point of Service 2. The overhead at this point could possibly be described as one of Cardiff's better efforts, with plenty of pull-offs to ease the curve.

John White

On a summers day in 1960, BUT/Bruce Coachworks 270 has dropped its passengers at the Pengam terminus discharge point and is now negotiating the turning circle, which was built around a large oval-shaped traffic island. The Brains Beer advert shows to good effect the use of the crimson lake and cream livery colours. It was not until 1961 that the use of colours other than that of the livery were allowed. Pre-war council housing forms the backdrop.

D.A.Thompson

After completing the turning circle, BUT/East Lancs 230 waits to depart the Pengam terminus on a return journey to the city centre. The first departure (1955 timetable) from Pengam on Weekdays and Saturdays was 5:16am, with a ten/twelve-minute frequency thereafter until 10:45pm. On Saturdays the frequency was increased to every eight minutes from 3:00pm until 10:26pm. The design of the Brains Red Dragon advert was unique to this vehicle. *M. Gylee*

In a similar way to Services 1 and 3, trolleybuses on Service 2, upon reaching the western end of Queen Street travelled inwards to the St. Mary Street terminus via St. John Street, The Hayes and Mill Lane. This 1960 view shows BUT/East Lancs 221 negotiating the Monument Roundabout on an inward journey. *R.F. Mack, courtesy NTA 1963*

SERVICE 3
ST. MARY STREET - ROATH PARK

Outward via St. Mary Street - High Street - Duke Street - Queen Street - Newport Road - City Road - Albany Road - Ninian Road. Inward via reverse of above route to Queen Street, then via Queen Street - St. John Street - Working Street - The Hayes - Mill Lane - St. Mary Street.

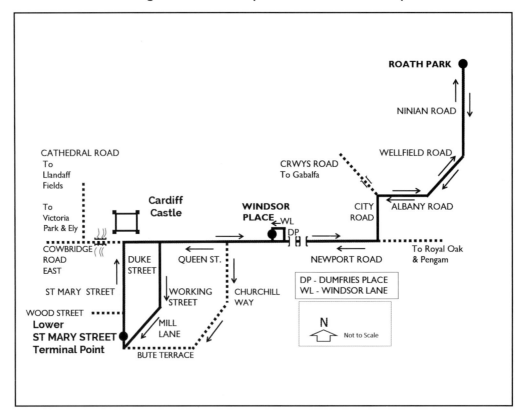

Trolleybus operation commenced Sunday December 4th 1949, replacing tram services 4A and 4B. The length of the route was 2.56 mile. Service 3 served the inner-city area of Roath before reaching the rather select district of Pen-y-Lan and terminating at Roath Park. The last day of trolleybus operation was Saturday 27th April 1968. Replaced the following day by oil-buses, the service being renumbered 58/59 and extended approximately one mile to Rhydypennau Cross Roads.

With bodywork constructed by local firm Bruce Coachworks on East Lancs frames, BUT 256 is seen waiting at the St. Mary Street terminal point of Service 3 before departing on its next journey to Roath Park in 1966. *Colin Hewlett*

In a busy St. Mary Street at its junction with Wood Street, BUT/East Lancs 227 is on an outward trip to Roath Park in December 1967. The framework holding its Christmas illuminations has obscured the destination box, and consequently a plate (hung beneath the near-side windscreen) acts instead as the route indicator. Following on behind, is a 1963 Leyland/East Lancs Leyland PD3 working on former trolleybus Service 2.

John White

At Castle junction, turning out of High Street into Duke Street during the summer of 1967 is BUT/East Lancs 227 on an outward journey to Roath Park on Service 3. The Black Tower and south gate of Cardiff Castle are in the background.
M.J. Russell

The former Taff Vale Railway Bridge spanning Newport Road provides the backdrop to this view of BUT/East Lancs 286 ascending the incline into Queen Street on an inward journey from Roath Park in the summer of 1967. Until July 1965, trolleybuses operating short-workings from Gabalfa / Roath Park to Windsor Place, turned right at this junction into Dumfries Place (see page 46).
M.J. Russell

Working an inward journey from Roath Park, BUT/Bruce Coachworks 255 has come to grief overtaking AEC Regent V/East Lancs motorbus 377 at the power frog in Queen Street on 9th September 1963.
John White

A Sunday morning scene in Queen Street in October 1965 where BUT/Bruce Coachworks 263 is seen using its traction batteries to manoeuvre around roadworks involving the laying of new rubber pads to activate the traffic signals seen in the background. This work was in connection with the Queen Street One-way scheme.
Colin Hewlett

Overhead linesman Leslie English holds back the driver of BUT/East Lancs (Bridlington) 249 beneath the former Taff Vale Railway Bridge in Newport Road in January 1966, whilst repairs are carried out to the trolleyheads of 254. *Colin Hewlett*

Meanwhile, overhead linesman Brinley Jones has opened the emergency window to provide a platform to attend to the trolleyhead problem affecting 254.
Colin Hewlett

A wartime scene in City Road (looking north) on 6th April 1940. The fenders on Brush car No. 85 have been painted white to help make it more visible in the blackout. Of note, is the continuous white line painted along the centre of the road to help motorists during the hours of darkness. *H.B. Priestley. Courtesy National Tramway Museum*

Many years later at the same location as the previous photograph, BUT/Bruce Coachworks 251 passes The Rupperra public house in City Road, on an inward journey in June 1967. The Ruperra opened in 1893 and later became known as the Poets Corner. It closed in 2015 and was demolished later that same year. *M.J. Russell*

Trolleybus operation of routes 1 and 3 came to an end on a rather wet and dismal day (Saturday 27th April 1968), when BUT/East Lancs 277 and 283 were photographed working inward along City Road, near to its junction with Newport Road.
John White

This view taken on 25th April 1968 depicts BUT/East Lancs 286 coasting under the power frog at the northern end of City Road, to take the outer set of wires leading to Albany Road and Roath Park (the inner set of wires continuing to Gabalfa).
John White

BUT/East Lancs 220 on an outward journey to Roath Park, makes its way cautiously towards Albany Road from City Road, crossing the inbound wiring leading from Gabalfa on 4th February 1967.

John White

BUT/Bruce Coachworks 265 catches the early evening sunshine as it turns out of Wellfield Road into Albany Road inward from Roath Park on 23rd September 1967. Immediately behind 265 is the Globe Cinema which opened in 1912 and survived until closure in May 1985.

John White

BUT/East Lancs 285 is seen in Wellfield Road on an inward Service 3 on 29th March 1967. The tower of the United Reformed Church features prominently in the background. More recently, the roadway has been narrowed, and the pavements widened to facilitate the operation of out-door hospitality venues. *John White*

With Roath Park Recreational Ground as a backdrop, BUT/East Lancs 275 is seen in Ninian Road on an inward journey from Roath Park on 13th September 1967. 'The "Rec,' as it is called locally, at one time attracted vast crowds to watch local baseball teams play. *John White*

AEC/Northern Counties 206 is working an inward morning peak-hour special in Wellfield Road on 5th March 1962. The first Weekday departure from St. Mary Street in 1955 was 5:17am (5:00am from Roath Park), a 10/11-minute frequency then continued throughout the day until 10:55pm (a more frequent service operated from midday on Saturdays). On Sunday mornings a 30-minute frequency operated from 8:10am, increasing to every 15 minutes from 1:30pm until 10:45pm.

John White

40

BUT/Bruce Coachworks 274 on an inward journey from Roath Park is leaving Ninian Road and entering Wellfield Road in February 1968. It carries an advert for Jotham's, a high-class gentleman's tailoring business based in Cardiff.

John Wiltshire

BUT/East Lancs 284 is on its way to the Roath Park terminus (about half-a-mile distant) on 2nd March 1968. A reversing stub for short-workings was originally proposed at the road junction behind 284 (Ninian Road/Penylan Road), but not proceeded with.
John White

BUT/East Lancs 223 is seen in Ninian Road on Service 3 to the city centre on March 2nd 1968. Following close behind is 220 on learner driver duties. Little has changed at this location since this view was taken.
John White

BUT/East Lancs 287 approaches the power feeder at the northern end of Ninian Road whilst working an inward journey during early April 1968. The two traction posts supporting the feeder date from 1949, whereas the majority along Ninian Road originated from tramway days, and were strengthened in the late 1950s with steel rods welded to their bases.

M.J. Russell

BUT/Bruce Coachworks 271 negotiates the turning circle at the Roath Park terminus of Service 3 in early April 1968. The roundabout was constructed in 1951 for safety reasons, prior to which trolleybuses turned within the constricted width of the roadway at this junction.
M.J. Russell

BUT/East Lancs 212 awaits departure from the Roath Park (Ninian Road) terminus of Services 3 & 4 on June 9th 1965. The Roath Park area, with its tree-lined roads of Victorian and Edwardian houses, could well be described today as one of the more affluent parts of the city.
David Pearson

BUT/East Lancs 277 is shown turning from Queen Street into St. John Street, from where it will proceed through Working Street, The Hayes and Mill Lane, before reaching the Service 3 terminus in St. Mary Street, on 18th April 1967.

John White

BUT/Bruce Coachworks 271 negotiates the Bute Monument roundabout in St. Mary Street on 7th February 1967. The roundabout was built in 1951, with the stipulation that no traction posts were to be erected thereon. Special dispensation was received from the MOT to use 20ft. length bracket arms instead of the normal 16ft. The Monument was erected in honour of the Second Marquess of Bute. The junction is now controlled by traffic signals.

John White

BUT/Bruce Coachworks 257 is shown on a short-working in February 1965 at the eastern end of Queen Street, as it prepares to negotiate the hand-operated frog for entry to Dumfries Place. Short-workings operating from Gabalfa / Roath Park to Windsor Place (and vice versa) were quite common on Services 1 and 3 during peak periods and Saturdays up until July 1965, when the wiring in Windsor Place and Dumfries Place was removed following the withdrawal of Service 5.

Colin Hewlett

A busy Saturday afternoon scene in Dumfries Place with BUT/East Lancs 227 and an unidentified vehicle on short-workings from Gabalfa / Roath Park on 19th June 1965.

Colin Hewlett

AEC/Northern Counties 209 is seen entering Windsor Lane to take up duties on an evening peak-hour short-working to Gabalfa on June 4th 1965.
John White

AEC/Northern Counties 201 is seen turning left from Windsor Place into Queen Street whilst working an evening peak-hour short-working from Windsor Place to Roath Park on 4th June 1965. The dewirement was caused because the conductor released the frog handle too soon as the booms on 201 passed through the hand frog.
John White

SERVICE 4
ROATH PARK - LLANDAFF FIELDS

via Ninian Road – Albany Road – City Road – Newport Road – Queen Street – Castle Street – Cowbridge Road East – Llandaff Fields

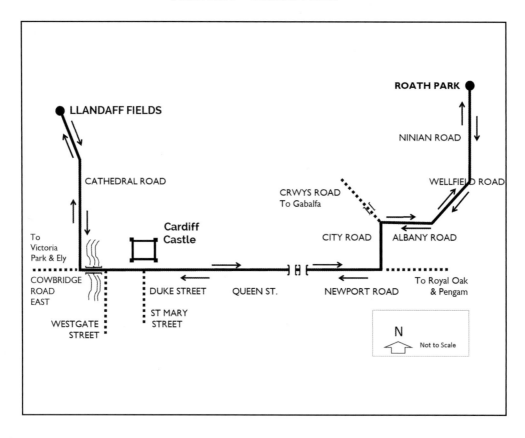

Cross-town trolleybus Service 4 commenced Sunday October 21st 1951. The length of the route was 3.73 miles. Both termini points were situated near extensive areas of parkland popular with the general public. Roath Park boasted a large boating lake, whilst an outdoor swimming pool at Llandaff Fields was very popular in the summer months. People travelling to these amenities provided good revenue for Service 4. The last day of trolleybus operation was 17th September 1966; replaced by oil-buses. The service was renumbered 55/56 and extended to operate to the then new Llanedeyrn housing estate.

BUT/East Lancs (Bridlington) 250 has just arrived at the discharge stop for Services 3 and 4 at the Roath Park terminus in Ninian Road, after a journey from Llandaff Fields in the summer of 1966. It will now pull forward to use the turning circle to reach the loading point on the opposite side of the road.
Author's Collection

Negotiating the traffic island at the junction of Ninian Road and Lake Road West on 20th December 1965 is BUT/Bruce Coachworks 251. It is carrying out the manoeuvre mentioned in the previous photograph. *John White*

A view of BUT/East Lancs 211 at the loading point of Service 4 in Ninian Road on September 16th 1966. The first Weekday departure from Roath Park in 1955 was 8:10am (8:5am from Llandaff Fields). Thereafter an 11/12-minute frequency continued throughout the day until 10:17pm. A generous 15-minute service operated on Sundays from 1:38pm until 10:17pm. *John White*

On a rather wet day - 19th June 1966, BUT/Bruce Coachworks 269 is seen in Ninian Road passing Roath Park Recreational Ground on its way to Roath Park. This scene remains much the same today.
Peter Mitchell

On its way to Roath Park in the summer of 1962, AEC/Northern Counties 205 is passing Thomas & Evans grocery shop in Wellfield Road. Many of the shops in the background are using sun blinds to protect their products on display in the windows.
CTPG

Bristol K6A tower wagon No. 3 (former oil-bus No. 83) is seen in June 1966 assisting in the replacement of the worn positive running wire in Wellfield Road (with wire formerly used in Lower Cathedral Road). *CTPG*

BUT/Bruce Coachworks 271 is travelling along Albany Road towards Roath Park in August 1966. Today, this area is densely populated by students, and many of the traditional style shops seen in the background have been replaced by fast food outlets. *R. F. Mack, courtesy NTA (1963)*

Turning out of Albany Road into City Road, BUT/East Lancs 229 is on its way to Llandaff Fields in August 1966. The wiring leading off to the left was used by Services 1 and 9 to reach Gabalfa. The wiring in City Road was used by routes 1,3,4 and 9.

R. F. Mack, courtesy NTA (1963)

BUT/East Lancs 229 is seen in City Road, Roath, at its junction with St. Peter's Street, working a Service 4 journey towards Roath Park in 1966. The showroom of N. W. Nash Ltd., the main Cardiff agent for Vauxhall cars can be seen on the left. The spire of St. James Church (now closed) in Newport Road can be seen in the distance. *R. F. Mack, Courtesy NTA (1963)*

AEC/Northern Counties 209 is shown turning out of City Road into Newport Road, travelling to Llandaff Fields on 27th August 1962. It survived in service until December of that year before being withdrawn and sold for scrap. There was a full triangular overhead layout at this junction, and overhead equipment included three cross-overs, two hand-operated frogs, three trailing frogs and one power frog.

John White

53

Roadworks to transform Newport Road into a dual carriageway were taking place when this view of BUT/East Lancs 228, on Service 4 to Llandaff Fields was taken in May 1965. As the roadworks proceeded, the trolleybus overhead wiring was repositioned accordingly (witness the redundant single-line hangers still attached to the span wire).   *M. Gylee*

BUT/Bruce Coachworks 271 working on Service 4 to Roath Park, has just passed under the former Rhymney Railway and Taff Vale Railway Bridges in Newport Road during April 1965. Cardiff Corporation Bruce Coachworks bodied Bristol KW6G oil-bus 125 and Western Welsh Weymann bodied Leyland Olympian 1213 complete the picture.   *M. Gylee*

BUT/East Lancs 216 is seen at the junction of Queen Street and Dumfries Place, travelling east, and approaching the former Taff Vale Railway Bridge in Newport Road during July 1965. The crossover was in the process of being removed as part of the wiring alterations required for the introduction of the Queen Street one-way scheme later that year. The imposing frontage to the former Taff Vale Railway Chief Offices (demolished 1973) is on the right.

John White

Making its way east along Queen Street on a Sunday afternoon in January 1962 is BUT/East Lancs 218. It is travelling on the wrong side of the road in order to pass a Foden cement mixer lorry making a delivery to the building site once occupied by the Gaumont Cinema.

CTPG

After passing through a section isolator, BUT/East Lancs 222 glides along Duke Street making its way to Llandaff Fields on 6th July 1966. Following 222 is a Leyland Royal Tiger saloon belonging to Red & White Services. This is still a recognisable scene today, although the number of traffic lanes in each direction has been reduced to one, and Queen Street (in the background) is now pedestrianised.

John White

With parts of the Roman-built Castle Wall visible in the background, BUT/Bruce Coachworks 274 passes from Duke Street into Castle Street on its way to Llandaff Fields on 19th June 1966. There was a full triangular overhead layout at this junction, held aloft by traction posts painted ivory to help make them blend better with their surroundings.

Peter Mitchell

With the Castle Clocktower providing the backdrop, BUT/East Lancs 222 passes through Castle Street at its junction with Westgate Street, travelling to Llandaff Fields on July 6th 1966. 222 was the last trolleybus to retain its front exit door, a feature it retained until withdrawal in October 1966.

BUT/East Lancs 211 is about to turn left from Cathedral Road into Cowbridge Road East on its way to Roath Park. Period British style ' No Waiting' signs and a blue police telephone box add extra interest to this Summer 1966 view. Thankfully, the avenue of trees still remains, and the scene is easily recognisable today.   *M. J. Russell*

This photograph was taken on 17th September 1966, the last day of trolleybus operation on Service 4. One of the vehicles chosen to operate on that day was BUT/East Lancs 280, which had re-entered service only three days earlier following a repaint. It is seen in Cathedral Road on a journey from Llandaff Fields to Roath Park.   *John White*

Brush tram No. 14 built in 1925, is in Cathedral Road working on route 1 (Llandaff Fields – Whitchurch Road) on 7th April 1938. In the back ground, The Westgate public house owned by Brains Brewery is prominent on the corner of Cowbridge Road and Lower Cathedral Road.   *H.B. Priestly Courtesy of the National Tramway Museum*

Viewed some twenty-eight years later in 1966, at the same location (Cathedral Road) as the previous photograph, BUT/ East Lancs 229 is working towards Llandaff Fields on Service 4. Many of the large Victorian houses along this road were built originally for ship owners and coal exporters. Today, they often sell for amounts well in excess £1,500,000.

R.F. Mack courtesy of NTA

BUT/Bruce Coachworks 274 is seen in Cathedral Road bound for Roath Park on 19th June 1966. The scene here looks much the same today, although the Presbyterian Church in the background has since closed for worship, with its interior now converted for office use. *Peter Mitchell*

BUT/East Lancs 222 has almost reached the end of Cathedral Road as it prepares to enter Llandaff Fields turning circle in May 1966. A passenger stands on its open platform, eagerly awaiting arrival at the terminus. *John White*

With some of the mature trees at the Llandaff Fields terminus as a backdrop, BUT/East Lancs 215 is seen negotiating the 'trolleybuses only' turning circle during June 1965. Annual rent of £15 was paid to the Parks Department for use of the land as a turning point. The turning circle roadway remains in use today, but as a pay and display carpark. *Colin Hewlett*

A view taken during the removal of the trolleybus overhead at Llandaff Fields turning circle in December 1966.
Colin Hewlett

SERVICE 5
WINDSOR PLACE - VICTORIA PARK

via Windsor Place – Queen Street – Duke Street – Cowbridge Road East

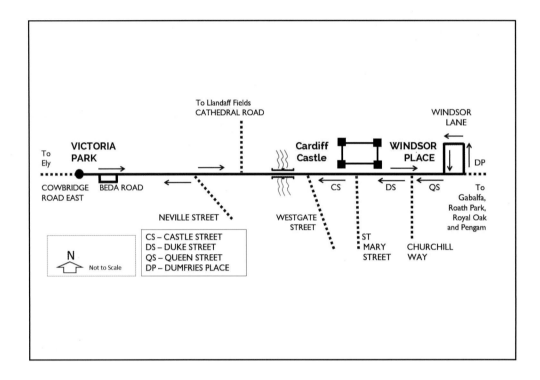

Trolleybus service commenced Sunday 4th July 1948, replacing temporarily oil-bus operated tram route No. 8, trams being withdrawn from the route on 24th January 1948. The length of the route was 2.21 miles. Service 5 could possibly be described as a short-working of Service 8. After leaving its city centre terminus, Service 5 travelled through the busy Queen Street shopping area, and then onwards along Cowbridge Road East (with its wide variety of shops) to Victoria Park. The service was well-used by office workers and shoppers during the day, and by people coming into the city centre to visit the cinemas and public houses in the evening.

The last day of trolleybus operation was Saturday 24th July 1965. There was no direct replacement service.

The city centre terminus of Service 5 was located at the eastern end of Queen Street, and took the form of an anti-clockwise turning loop comprising Queen Street, Dumfries Place (discharge point), Windsor Lane (loading point) and Windsor Place. This view shows BUT/Bruce Coachworks 261 about to turn from Queen Street into Dumfries Place in June 1965.

John White

As BUT/East Lancs 215 enters Dumfries Place in June 1965, it passes John Collier gentlemen's outfitting shop (now in use as a Sainsbury supermarket). All other properties in this view have since been demolished, whilst Dumfries Place has been widened and is now a six-lane dual carriageway. The discharge point for Service 5 was situated just out of camera-shot to the right. *Author's Collection*

On 9th March 1965, BUT/East Lancs (Bridlington) 249 is about to enter Windsor Lane, where the boarding point for Service 5 was located. *M.J. Russell*

BUT/Bruce Coachworks 262 at the Windsor Lane boarding point in June 1965. The first departure from this point (1955 timetable) on Weekdays and Saturdays was 8:01am, thereafter a 10/12-minute frequency continued until 11:00pm. A 12-minute frequency operated on Sundays from 1:30pm until 10:40pm. *Author's Collection*

BUT/East Lancs 225 is attempting to turn from Windsor Lane into Windsor Place on a journey to Victoria Park in February 1965. Inconsiderate parking by the driver of a British Road Services vans is causing a problem, and a member of the public is assisting the trolleybus driver with the manoeuvre. *Colin Hewlett*

BUT/East Lancs 230 is seen turning out of Windsor Place into Queen Street on its way to Victoria Park in June 1965. The hand-operated facing frog just behind 230 was used by Services 1 and 3 making the left turn into Queen Street on short-workings to Gabalfa and Roath Park. *Author's Collection*

On its way to Victoria Park, BUT/East Lancs 218 passes through Castle Street junction in 1961. To the rear of 218, an unidentified trolleybus on Service 9 is about to turn into High Street from Duke Street. *M. Gylee*

BUT/East Lancs (Bridlington) 247 is in Castle Street, working Service 5 to Dumfries Place in August 1964. Part of the Clock Tower of Cardiff Castle forms the backdrop in this view.   *John Wiltshire*

BUT/East Lancs 228 is seen in Cowbridge Road East at its junction with Beda Road, on Service 5 to Windsor Place in May 1965. At the time this view was taken, trolleybus Services 5, 5A/B, 8 and 10A/B all operated along this section of Cowbridge Road East, and provided a very frequent service throughout the day   *M.Gylee*

BUT/East Lancs (Bridlington) 246 is leaving the discharge point at Victoria Park terminus in the summer of 1964, and is ready to use the turning circle to arrive at the loading point on the opposite side of the road. There is a good display of products outside the local ironmonger's shop. *Colin Hewlett*

BUT/Bruce Coachworks 252 is seen waiting at the loading point of Service 5 at Victoria Park in March 1965. An overhead passing loop allowed inbound trolleybuses working on the 10A/B services to overtake Service 5 vehicles. *C. Carter*

SERVICE 5A/B
VICTORIA PARK - WOOD STREET

5A Victoria Park – Wood Street
via Cowbridge Road East - Castle Street – High Street - St. Mary Street - Wood Street. Return: via Tudor Road - Clare Street - Neville Street - Cowbridge Road East. Length of the route was 2.03 miles.

5B Victoria Park – Wood Street
via Cowbridge Road East - Neville Street - Clare Street - Tudor Road - Wood Street. Return: via St. Mary Street – High Street - Castle Street - Cowbridge Road East. Length of the route was 2.05 miles.

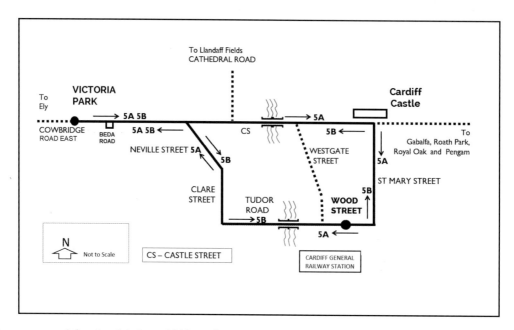

Services 5A/B commenced Sunday 6th June 1948, replacing tram routes No. 5A/B. The service was drastically cut-back from September 1953 to operate on Weekdays during peak-hour periods only, with some short workings operating to Beda Road. A special Sunday morning service operated between 6:15am and 1:00pm on a 30-minute frequency, which remained until the route closed in 1965. The official last day of trolleybus operation was Saturday 24th July 1965; although the services had not operated after 22nd July 1965 due to a shortage of staff; there was no direct replacement service.

Awaiting departure from Victoria Park in May 1965 is AEC/Northern Counties 201.

M. Gylee

The 5A/B routes diverged at St. David's Hospital junction to form two loops in order to reach the Wood Street terminus. This view shows BUT/Bruce Coachworks 262 leaving Cowbridge Road East and about to enter Neville Street on a 5B working to Wood Street in May 1965. It would return to this junction via St. Mary Street, Castle Street and Cowbridge Road East. Trolleybuses working Service 5A operated in the converse direction.

Author's Collection

BUT/Bruce Coachworks 253 is at the junction of Neville Street, Clare Street and Lower Cathedral Road, working an inbound journey on route 5B in May 1965. The wiring to the right leads into Lower Cathedral Road. *Author's Collection*

BUT/Bruce Coachworks 254 turns out of Clare Street into Tudor Road, working inwards to Wood Street during early June 1965. *CTPG*

AEC/Northern Counties 204 is seen arriving at the Wood Street terminus of Service 5B on February 19th 1964. Substancial redevelopment in recent years has transformed the landscape at this point, and although Wood Street still exists, all buildings in this view have been swept away and replaced with new high-rise office blocks which lack any real character.

David Pearson

At the same location as the previous view, but looking in the opposite direction, AEC/Northen Counties 201 is shown double-parked at the 5A terminal point, prior to working an outward journey to Victoria Park in November 1963. In the background, a Rhondda Transport AEC Regent V with MCW Orion bodywork is seen leaving the Central Bus Station on a journey to the Rhondda Valleys.

CTPG

A busy scene on a Rugby International Saturday and BUT/Bruce Coachworks 271 is in Castle Street working inbound in December 1964. It will shortly turn right into High Street and then continue to the terminus in Wood Street via St. Mary Street. The destination blind on 271 is incorrectly set for Service 5B, whereas it should be displaying 5A.

Author's Collection

A schoolboy signals with his hand to the driver of AEC/Northern Counties 201 to stop, as it approaches Cardiff Bridge on an outbound 5B trip to Victoria Park in April 1964.

Colin Hewlett

A scene at the junction of Neville Street and Lower Cathedral Road on 15th May 1966. Two overhead linesmen are seen removing the screws clamping the grooved trolley wire to the 'ear', thus enabling the wire to be wound-in for further use elsewhere on the system.

Colin Hewlett

Taken at the same location and day as the previous view, Bristol K6A tower wagon No.3 is parked in Lower Cathedral Road after winding in redundant trolley wire in Lower Cathedral Road. The wire was later reused in Wellfield Road.

Colin Hewlett

SERVICE 6/6A
LLANDAFF FIELDS – PIER HEAD (DOCKS)

Service 6A Wood St. - Clarence Rd. commenced Sunday 1st March 1942 replacing tram route No. 6A Wood St. – Clarence Rd. The route was as follows: via Wood St. - Tudor Rd. – Clare Rd. - Corporation Rd. - Clarence Rd. Return: via reverse of above route to Wood St. The length of the route was 1.86 miles. This was Cardiff's first trolleybus service.

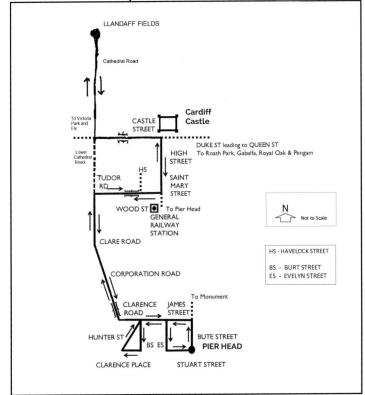

Service 6 Llandaff Fields - Clarence Rd. commenced Sunday 8th November 1942, replacing tram route No. 6 Llandaff Fields – Wood St. The new service interworked with existing trolleybus Service 6A Wood St. - Clarence Road. The length of the route was 3.35 miles. From Sunday 17th August 1947, the 6 and 6A were extended from Clarence Rd. to the Pier Head.

Commencing Sunday 2nd November 1947, Services 6 and 6A merged to become Service 6 Llandaff Fields – Pier Head, the length of the route was 3.58 miles.

Not all destination blinds were amended to show these route number changes, and 6A continued to be displayed on some trolleybuses until the route finished in 1966.

Because of a weight restriction imposed on Wood St. Bridge, trolleybuses were replaced by oil-buses on the Wood St. - Pier Head section commencing Friday 17th December 1965 (trolleybuses continuing to operate the section of route between Llandaff Fields and Wood St.). Oil-buses replaced trolleybuses on the remaining Wood St. - Llandaff Fields section commencing Sunday 17th April 1966.

BUT/East Lancs 277 is awaiting passengers at the terminus of Service 6 in the parkland setting of Llandaff Fields on 4th July 1956. Service 6 was a busy cross-city route passing through Canton, the city centre and Grangetown on its way to the Docks
Peter Mitchell

Shortly after leaving the Llandaff Fields terminus, BUT/East Lancs 224 is seen at the junction of Cathedral Road and Penhill Road on 28th January 1966. The original proposal was to turn trolleybuses within the constricted width of this junction, but as Ministry approval was not forthcoming, a turning circle was constructed within the entrance to Llandaff Fields.

John White

AEC/Northern Counties 203 is in Cathedral Road on its way to the Pier Head on 12th February 1954. This vehicle is now preserved by the BTS, and operates at the Sandtoft Trolleybus Museum. Just visible are tarred-over tramway tracks last used in 1942, and which were not finally removed until November 1961.

Derek Chaplin (courtesy Peter Brabham)

On an overcast winters day in early December 1965, BUT/East Lancs (Bridlington) 249 is about to turn right from Castle Street into High Street on Service 6. Passing on the inside lane is BUT/Bruce Coachworks 262, which has been fitted with an illuminated disc for the Christmas period. Note the temporary destination board placed in the upper-deck front window of 262.

Colin Hewlett

On its way to the Pier Head, BUT/Bruce Coachworks 260 is seen in Wood Street on July 6th 1958. It still retains the front exit door, but it would no longer be in use. Some interesting period cars are to be seen in the background.

Author's Collection

In June 1963, BUT/East Lancs 275 is approaching the Service 6 timing-point in Wood Street, on its way to Llandaff Fields. The 1951 timetable shows the first departure on Weekdays and Saturdays from Llandaff Fields at 5:35am, thereafter a morning/afternoon frequency of every 10/14 minutes. An infrequent Sunday morning service operated from

AEC/Northern Counties 206 is in Wood Street operating a journey on Service 6 to the Pier Head, circa 1949. As 'Llandaff Fields' was not available on the destination blinds of the AEC trolleybuses, 'Cathedral Road' was displayed instead. During wartime, these vehicles often carried in excess of 100 passengers on journeys between Wood Street and Clarence Road (mainly workers at Currans Munition Factory situated adjacent to the Clarence Road terminus).

Don Jones EATMS

BUT/East Lancs 216 is seen crossing Wood Street Bridge on its way to the Pier Head in April 1965. It has just passed the Wales Empire Swimming Pool (on the left in this view), opened in 1958 for the Sixth British Empire Games that were held in Cardiff that year. The pool has since closed and was demolished in 1998. An entertainment complex now occupies the site.   *M. Gylee*

BUT/East Lancs 226 is travelling over Wood Street Bridge in the opposite direction to that of 216 shown above, in April 1965. Tubular suspension was used to support the wiring across the bridge.   *M. Gylee*

AEC/Northern Counties 202 is in Clare Road heading for the Pier Head, circa 1950. Visible in the background is the overhead wiring used for accessing Clare Road Depot (closed in October 1953). *John Wiltshire*

A somewhat atmospheric view of BUT/East Lancs 222 in Corporation Road, Grangetown, on its way to the Pier Head, circa 1949. Tubular suspension was used throughout the entire length of Corporation Road, and was erected by Clough, Smith Ltd. in 1941. Three men cycling home from work, probably from somewhere in the docks area, captures the period well. *John Wiltshire*

BUT/Bruce Coachworks 269 emerges from the steel girder work of Clarence Road Bridge, as it works a Service 6 journey to Llandaff Fields in 1962. The bridge was closed to traffic for six months in 1959 to enable repairs to the wind-bracing girders to be undertaken. During the closure period, the original wooden troughing supporting the trolley wire, was replaced by twin-line hangers and porcelain insulators, attached direct to the wind bracing girders.

An evenly spaced curve has been achieved in the overhead wiring leading from Evelyn Street into Stuart Street, where BUT/East Lancs 228 is depicted in August 1960. The wiring was extended from Clarence Road to the Pier Head in August 1947. This is 'real' dockland territory, with plenty of character, but sadly everything in this view has now disappeared.

D.A.Thompson

The conductor of BUT/East Lancs 217 is seen taking a well-earned break at the Pier Head terminus in the summer of 1960. During the P.A.Y.E. period (1942 – 1950), the conductor would use a seat situated just below where the used ticket box is mounted (behind the conductor's head in this view) to ensure that passengers boarding placed their penny in the coin receptacle. *M. Gylee*

James Street (Docks) One-way Scheme, Routes 6/9

A new one-way traffic scheme in the Docks area affecting Services 6 and 9 commenced 21st September 1964. The terminal point of both routes was relocated from the west side of Bute Street to the east side. On 28th June 1965 BUT/East Lancs 224 is overtaking similar vehicle 218 at the revised terminal point in Bute Street. *Hugh Taylor*

BUT/East Lancs 222 has just turned from Bute Street into Stuart Street whilst working an NTA tour of the Cardiff system on Sunday 20th March 1966. Note that the bracket arm still has two (redundant) Bowstring brackets attached, a reminder of the days when the single-deck trolleys once used this part of Stuart Street. The positive raked traction post (to the rear of 222) is planted adjacent to the sea wall.

John White

The direction of traffic in Evelyn Street was also reversed to comply with the new one-way scheme. This view shows BUT/ East Lancs 215 in Evelyn Street approaching the junction with James Street in March 1965.

C. Carter

Weight Restriction on Wood Street Bridge, 6/9 Routes

On 16th December 1965 an emergency weight restriction order was placed on Wood Street Bridge. The following day, the 6 and 9 Services were truncated to a stopping place in Central Square (General Station), where passengers transferred to a replacement oil-bus service operating to the Pier Head (and vice versa) to complete their journeys. BUT/East Lancs (Bridlington) 249 is operating a short-working from Llandaff Fields to the General Station and is about to turn right from Castle Street into High Street on 24th February 1966. During the period of short-workings, the normal full destination display was still used, however, at times the conductor would create an incorrect version, as shown in this view.   *John White*

BUT/Bruce Coachworks 273 is operating on a short working from Llandaff Fields and is turning from Wood Street into Central Square on 9th April 1966.   *John White*

The short-workings on Services 6 and 9 continued until 17th April 1966, when sufficient vehicles were available to convert both services to oil-buses. BUT/Bruce Coachworks 274 leaves Central Square and is turning into Wood Street on its return journey to Llandaff Fields on the last day of trolleybus operation on these routes (16th April 1966). The wires on the far right were used by outward trolleybuses leaving Havelock Street on Services 10A/B.   *John White*

The wiring in Lower Cathedral Road was retained as an emergency diversion route for Services 4 and 6, but was generally used for only two hours once a year, on the day of the annual Miner's Parade through the city centre. This view shows BUT/East Lancs 223 using battery power to cross from Cathedral Road into Lower Cathedral Road, at the junction with Cowbridge Road East on 19th June 1965.

John White

Taken on the same day as the photograph above, BUT/East Lancs 226 is viewed at the opposite end of Lower Cathedral Road, and has just left Clare Street. This was the last occasion on which the wiring in Lower Cathedral Road was used for diversionary purposes.

John White

CARDIFF CORPORATION TRANSPORT DEPARTMENT (TROLLEYBUS SECTION)

TROLLEY BUS OPERATION

Service No. 6 CATHEDRAL ROAD, WOOD STREET & CLARENCE ROAD.

The Public are notified that commencing **SUNDAY, 1st. MARCH 1942,** Trolley Buses will be substituted for Trams on the **No. 6A Service serving Wood Street - Clarence Road.**

The fare for the journey Wood Street to Clarence Road will be **ONE PENNY ONLY.**

The **"PAY AS YOU ENTER"** system of fare collection will operate on this Service. Passengers will be required to have the exact fare of **ONE PENNY** ready before boarding, and it will facilitate loading if passengers for the lower deck board on the left and passengers for the upper deck on the right side of the platform. Separate slots are provided and lower deck passengers should place the coin in the slot on the left with the right hand. Upper deck passengers should use the left hand to place the coin in the slot on the right of the collecting box.

TICKETS WILL NOT BE ISSUED, CHANGE WILL NOT BE GIVEN, AND PASSENGERS MUST HAVE THE EXACT FARE READY BEFORE ENTERING THE TROLLEYBUS.

ONE FARE ONLY - ONE PENNY

For Timetable arrangements, see handbills hung in Trams serving the Cathedral Road and Grangetown Areas, or enquire from the Central Offices, Womany Street (Tel. No. 7940, Extension 287).

February 1942   2/42 W.M. 7   J. W. DUNNING, M.Iinst. T.,
                                                                                 Traffic Manager.

The introduction of trolleybus Service 6A on 1st March 1942 saw the inauguration of a P.A.Y.E. fare system with adults and children paying a universal fare of just one penny, with no change being given or tickets issued. A coin receptacle mounted on the staircase stringer allowed passengers to insert their penny coin as they passed by (official statistics showed a boarding time of one second per passenger). The P.A.Y.E. fare system was extended gradually to all tram/trolleybus services and several oil-bus routes. In the post-war period, rising costs of fuel, wages and materials saw the one penny fare increased to a penny half-penny in June 1949. With a huge accumulated deficit, it was decided in 1950 to abandon the flat fare system, and replace it with a variable fare structure, the final day of PA.Y.E. operation being 10th November 1950. Service 6 offered the longest distance you could travel for 1d (3.58 miles).

Cardiff Corporation Transport Dept.

Pay
As
You
Enter!

VERY SOON . . .

the Tram Service serving the Cathedral Road area will be replaced by Trolley Buses. The new Service will operate as an extension of the present Service between Clarence Road and Wood Street.

The Fare for the through journey from Cathedral Road to Clarence Road will be **ONE PENNY ONLY.**

The "PAY AS YOU ENTER" system of fare collection, which has proved so successful on the Clarence Road section, will be extended to the new Service. In order that passengers may become conversant with the P.A.Y.E. system, and so assist in affording a more economic and efficient service, a number of hints for their guidance are shown on the back hereof.

(See over).

SERVICE 8
ROYAL OAK - VICTORIA PARK

via Newport Road – Queen Street – Castle Street – Cowbridge Road East

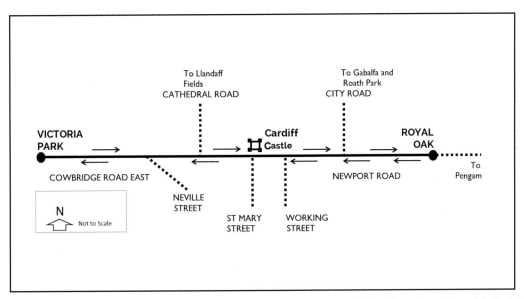

Service 8 Pengam - Victoria Park Trolleybus service commenced Sunday October 15th 1950, replacing temporarily oil-bus operated tram route No. 8 Victoria Park – Newport Road. Operation confined to Weekday early mornings and Sundays. Length of the route was 4.05 miles.

Service revised commencing Sunday October 21st 1951 to **Service 8 Royal Oak – Victoria Park.** Length of the route was 3.05 miles. On weekdays, some morning and evening peak hour journeys commenced and terminated at the Pengam terminus of Service 2.

The last day of trolleybus operation was Saturday 17th February 1968. The replacement oil-bus service carried the same route number, and the route was extended from The Royal Oak eastwards to Dorchester Avenue.

BUT/ Bruce Coachworks 271 is approaching the power frog located just before the Royal Oak turning circle. After negotiating the circle, 271 will come to rest at the boarding point for route 8, on the opposite side of the road, where intending passengers can be seen waiting its arrival.
C. Carter

Negotiating the traffic island forming the Royal Oak turning circle is BUT/Bruce Coachworks 272 in June 1962. Unfortunately, it seems that the driver of 272 has not operated the frog correctly. The conductor (busy re-poling 272 onto the correct wiring), has set an incorrect destination display, as the one shown is for route 8 journeys extending beyond the Royal Oak to Pengam. *Author*

BUT/East Lancs 215 awaits its next journey on Service 8 at the Royal Oak terminus on 15th February 1968, two days before trolleybus operation of the route ceased. The passing loop allowed trolleybuses travelling inwards from Roath Depot to the city centre to overtake trolleybuses awaiting their departure time from the terminus. A new, much smaller style destination blind had recently been fitted to 215. In anticipation of Service 8 being the next trolleybus route to be abandoned, it was thus omitted from the new blind, hence the metal destination plate placed in the driver's windscreen.

John White

89

In this view BUT/East Lancs 227 is about to complete the turning circle at the Royal Oak on 2nd February 1968, prior to entering the passing loop at the terminus. Prominent in the background is the public house from which the terminal point derives its name.

R. Helliar-Symons

BUT/East Lancs 227 is pictured at the curve in Newport Road opposite Roath Court Funeral Home on Sunday 3rd September 1967. It is passing ex-Glasgow Corporation BUT/Burlingham TBS 21 which had de-wired negotiating the curve during a tour of the system.

David Pearson

Newport Road is the scene of this view of BUT/Bruce Coachworks 265 heading towards the city centre on 9th September 1967. The cross-city route 8 connected the east of the city to the west, and vice versa. It was a busy service, and the first Weekday departure from the Royal Oak was 5:38am, with an 8/10-minute frequency thereafter until 10:45pm (1955 Timetable).

John White.

BUT/East Lancs 212 is busy picking-up passengers from the Queen's Arcade stop in Queen Street, whilst working west bound on Service 8 to Victoria Park on 28th June 1965. AEC/Northern Counties 204, which is travelling from Roath Depot to Havelock Street to take-up duties on Service 10A, patiently waits for 212 to proceed on its way. Queen Street at this time was Cardiff's main shopping area. *Hugh Taylor*

BUT/East Lancs 221 with booms out-stretched, heads a line-up of traffic in Duke Street, whilst working on Service 8 from Victoria Park to the Royal Oak in March 1965. *Colin Hewlett*

Following a heavy shower of rain, BUT/East Lancs (Bridlington) 246 is leaving Duke Street to enter Castle Street on 14th August 1963. Trolleybus drivers always travelled through this full triangular overhead junction at a very slow speed for fear of de-wiring. Except for Services 10A/B and 16, all Cardiff trolleybus routes passed through this junction.

John White

An evening peak hour view of BUT/East Lancs 279 heading east and about to leave Castle Street and enter Duke Street. The outer set of wiring was used by Service 6 trolleybuses to turn right into High Street. *John White*

Travelling west along Castle Street at its junction with Westgate Street is BUT/East Lancs 213 on April 26th 1966 It is just about to pass through the inbound wires of Services 10A/B. The octagon tower (built 1439) of Cardiff Castle is on the extreme left, the spire being added in 1875. *John White*

BUT/Bruce Coachworks 271 is heading west across Cardiff Bridge on its way to Victoria Park on 4th February 1967. Meanwhile, BUT/East Lancs 275 is passing-by inbound on Service 10A, its driver preparing to operate the power frog just ahead, for the right-hand turn into Westgate Street.

John White

Traffic builds up behind BUT/Bruce Coachworks 262, as it picks up passengers in Cowbridge Road East, Canton, on its way to Victoria Park, on 2nd February 1968. Meanwhile, BUT 252 (with similar bodywork), is travelling eastbound to the Royal Oak on a Service 8 duty. *R. Helliar-Symons*

Taken in the summer of 1964, this view shows BUT/East Lancs 285 proceeding west along Cowbridge Road East, Canton, at its junction with Neville Street (used by Services 5A/B). In the background is the Wyndham public house (closed in 1994). *M. Gylee*

A little further along Cowbridge Road East, BUT/East Lancs 275 is on its way to Victoria Park, and approaching the junction with Leckwith Road, Canton, on 2nd February 1968.
R. Helliar-Symons

The trading name of George Mason was once very familiar on the high streets of most large towns.

Travelling along Cowbridge Road East approaching Victoria Park terminus is BUT/East Lancs 213 on 18th April 1967. It has taken power to operate the facing-frog for the outer set of wires leading to the turning circle (the inner set of wires serving Services 10A/B to Ely). Victoria Park was opened in 1897 to celebrate Queen Victoria's Diamond Jubilee.

John White

The steering on BUT/East Lancs 215 is on full lock as it negotiates the Victoria Park turning circle on 15th February 1968. When the turning circle was constructed (in 1948), a section of the park was acquired to ease the constricted width of the roadway, but turning at this point still remained a tight manoeuvre. *John White*

In this view, BUT/East Lancs 227 is about to enter the lay-by at Victoria Park Terminus in May 1966. The overhead line coming in from Ely (10A/B) can be seen joining the trailing frog to the rear of 227. *Colin Hewlett*

Roath Court Wiring Alterations 1969

A few months after the withdrawal of trolleybus Service 8 (in February 1968), roadworks commenced in Newport Road at the junction with Albany Road (Roath Court). This work involved alterations to the overhead wiring in the easterly direction, and the repositioning of several traction posts. The new wiring was brought into use on Sunday January 26th 1969, although by this time the wiring was only being used by trolleybuses returning to Roath Depot out of service.

This view shows new overhead trolley wire being erected at Roath Court on 6th October 1968.   *CTPG*

A linesman is seen securing the new trolley wire temporarily to a traction post in Newport Road on 6th October 1968. Although by this time the days of the trolleybus system were numbered, it is interesting to note that the newly planted traction posts have been repainted. *CTPG*

A view taken at Roath Court looking east towards the Royal Oak on Saturday 25th January 1969. BUT/East Lancs 228 is on its way back to Roath Depot after working on the Ely services. It was standard practise for passengers to be carried on 'Depot only' journeys, and occasionally trolleybuses displayed Service 8 on their rear blinds, as in this instance.

John White

A view taken at the eastern point of the roadworks (where the new wiring ended), and which gives a much wider aspect of the alterations carried out to the overhead. BUT/East Lancs 281 is returning to Roath Depot on 25th January 1969.

John White

SERVICE 9
GABALFA - PIER HEAD (DOCKS)

via Whitchurch Road – Crwys Road - City Road – Newport Road – Queen Street – St. Mary Street - Wood Street – Clare Road – Corporation Road - Clarence Road - Pier Head (Docks)

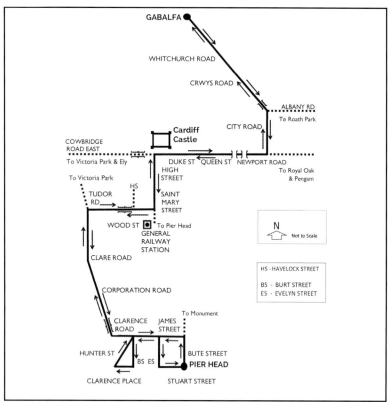

Trolleybus service 9 commenced Sunday October 21st 1951, linking Gabalfa (in north Cardiff) with the Docks area. The route travelled through The Heath, Cathays, Roath and Grangetown districts (all well-populated areas). On Weekdays and Saturdays, the first departure (1955 timetable) from Gabalfa Terminus was 7:15am, and thereafter every 10/11 minutes until 10:22pm. Journey time between Gabalfa and the Pier Head was about 33 minutes (depending on the time of day). It was the second busiest trolleybus service, as regards the number of passengers carried (the busiest was the 10A/B).

Because of a weight restriction imposed on Wood Street Bridge, trolleybuses were replaced by oil buses on the Wood Street - Pier Head section of the route commencing 17th December 1965 (trolleybuses continuing to operate the section of route Wood Street – Gabalfa). Commencing Sunday 17th April 1966, oil buses replaced trolleybuses on the remaining Wood Street - Gabalfa section.

Following an unexpected overnight snowfall, BUT/Bruce Coachworks 270 has just left the Gabalfa terminus of Service 9 and is in St. Marks Avenue about to turn left into Whitchurch Road on 14th April 1966.   John White

BUT/Bruce Coachworks 252 has just passed under a power-feeder (fed from Kames Place sub-station) in Whitchurch Road, heading towards Gabalfa on 24th February 1966. 252 was one of a small number of trolleybuses fitted in 1961 with ex London Transport Executive Q1 type boom bases. Following behind is BUT/Bruce Coachworks 258 working on Service 1.

John White

BUT/East Lancs 225 passes the stone wall surrounding Cathays Cemetery, whilst working on Service 9 to the Pier Head on 24th February 1966. The Cemetery, which covers 110 acres, was opened in 1859, and is the third largest in Great Britain.

John White

On 24th February 1966, BUT/East Lancs (Bridlington) 249 is about to leave Crwys Road and enter Whitchurch Road whilst working on Service 9 to Gabalfa.

John White

BUT/East Lancs 219 passes The Royal George public house as it leaves Crwys Road to enter City Road, on a journey from Gabalfa to the Pier Head in January 1965. Services 1 and 9 shared the wiring from Gabalfa terminus to this junction, whilst in City Road the wiring was shared between Services 1, 3, 4, and 9. The Royal George is still open and trading in 2023.

Authors Collection

BUT/East Lancs 279 crosses into Newport Road from City Road beneath a maze of overhead equipment on 5th March 1962. Many Cardiff trolleybuses at this time (including 279) featured distinctive painted advertisements on their side panels, with lettering in crimson or black against a cream background, such as this example for local brewer S.A. Brain & Co. Ltd.

John White

AEC/Northern Counties 201 is pictured leaving the 'Capitol Cinema' stop in Queen Street, working Service 9 to Gabalfa on 12th June 1962. The inner set of wires (used by Service 5) will shortly turn into Dumfries Place. The block of buildings shown on the left were demolished in 1987, and the site has since been redeveloped as the 'Capitol Centre'. *John White*

On a very drab and overcast day, BUT/Bruce Coachworks 252 turns from Wood Street into St. Mary Street on its way to Gabalfa, on 16th April 1966. The background in this view has changed beyond recognition, and the sole remaining building standing today is The Royal Hotel on the extreme right.

John White

BUT/East Lancs (Bridlington) 247 is turning from Duke Street into High Street on its way to the Pier Head in September 1962. From this point, Services 6 and 9 followed the same route through to the Pier Head. *Tony Belton*

BUT/East Lancs (Bridlington) 249 is pictured turning from St. Mary Street into Wood Street on a journey from Gabalfa to the Pier Head on 19th February 1966. It has a somewhat neglected look (different coloured mudguards and a gashed side panel) as a result of reduced maintenance to the trolleybus fleet. *David Pearson*

AEC/Northern Counties 205 bound for the Pier Head, has stopped at the timing-point for Service 9 in Wood Street, during the summer of 1962. Although by this time confined mainly for use during peak-hours, these vehicles could occasionally be found on all-day service, especially Saturdays. The Brains Brewery chimney in St. Mary Street is prominent in the background.

D.A.Thompson

With St. David's House office complex (now demolished) as the backdrop, BUT/East Lancs 213 is shown at the timing-point in Wood Street before continuing its journey to Gabalfa in the summer of 1962. *D.A.Thompson*

Just before crossing Wood Street Bridge (from the Grangetown direction), BUT/East Lancs 229 is passing The Royal Tudor public house in Tudor Road, whilst on driver training duties in April 1965. Trolleybus Services 6 and 9 used Tudor Road on their journeys to and from the Pier Head. The Royal Tudor closed in 1994 and apartments now occupy the site. *M. Gylee*

BUT/East Lancs 218 has just passed under Clare Road Railway Bridge on its way to the Pier Head in August 1960. Clare Road Trolleybus Depot (closed in 1953) was situated just out of camera-shot to the right. A full triangular overhead junction existed at this point to allow access to and from the Depot, the only reminders of this being the two extra-length traction posts in the background. *D.A.Thompson*

BUT/East Lancs 214 is travelling across the Clarence Road Swing-Bridge on a journey to Gabalfa, in 1964. The bridge was officially opened in 1890 by the Duke of Clarence and Avondale. The centre span originally opened to allow the passage of vessels navigating the River Taff. In May 1939 a Royal Order was obtained relieving the Corporation of this duty. *C. Carter*

BUT/East Lancs 214 leans to the curve as it turns from James Street into Evelyn Street in August 1963. It received a major rebuild in early 1961, when the rear destination box was converted to route number display only (the first trolleybus in the fleet to be so treated). Just visible in James Street is the White Heart public house (now closed). *CTPG*

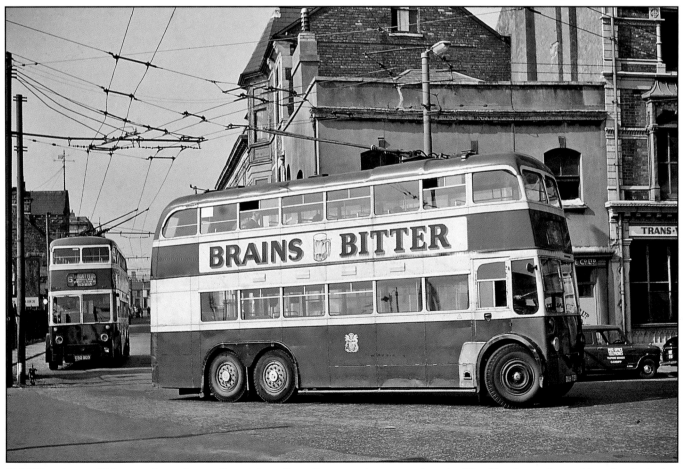

BUT/East Lancs 226 turns from Stuart Street into Bute Street as it approaches the Pier Head terminus of Service 9, during June 1963. Following closely behind is BUT/Bruce Coachworks 252 on Service 6. All other wiring in this view formed part of the reverser used by single-deck trolleybuses on Service 14. *M. Gylee*

Taken on the last day of single-deck trolleybus operation (11th January 1964), BUT/Bruce Coachworks 252 is at the Pier Head terminus waiting to depart on its next trip to Gabalfa. The insulating tape on the booms nearest to the trolley heads, has been painted white to aid drivers during a de-wirement at night-time. The experiment was short-lived. In the background single-deck BUT/East Lancs 242 is about to depart for The Monument.   *John White*

Facing the opposite way in Bute Street to the previous photograph, BUT/Bruce Coachworks 268 is awaiting departure time from the Pier Head for its next journey to Gabalfa in November 1962. Approaching the Pier Head is BUT/East Lancs 239. At the time this photograph was taken, the local Chamber of Trade was holding a 'Shopping Festival' event, the Transport Dept. participating by attaching flags to the booms on trolleybuses.   *Tony Belton*

Clarence Road Turning Facility

The original 'round-the-houses' turning facility at Clarence Road was retained for short-workings, etc. after Service 6 was extended to the Pier Head in August 1947. During April, May and June 1964, Services 6 and 9 were truncated to operate from this turning facility instead of the Pier Head because of roadworks in James Street. This view shows BUT/East Lancs 224 about to leave Clarence Road and enter Hunter Street in April 1964. *CTPG*

The same location as in the previous photograph, but this time looking out from Hunter Street into Clarence Road. BUT/East Lancs 222 is operating an NTA tour of the Cardiff system on 20th March 1966. Most of the BICC overhead equipment in this view dates from 1941. *John White*

The turning facility at Clarence Road saw little use in normal, quieter times but was ideal as a location for trainee drivers to receive instruction. BUT/Bruce Coachworks 269 is in Burt Street in 1963, along with driving instructor Fred Jones (on the far right). Clarence Place is to the left in this view.
M. Gylee

BUT/Bruce Coachworks 274 is leaving Hunter Street and entering Clarence Road in June 1964. The conductor has taken the lazy option of displaying just Gabalfa instead of a full route display showing intermediate points.
M. Gylee

SERVICE 10A/B

10A Havelock Street – Victoria Park – Green Farm Road via Grand Avenue
10B Havelock Street – Victoria Park – Green Farm Road via Cowbridge Road

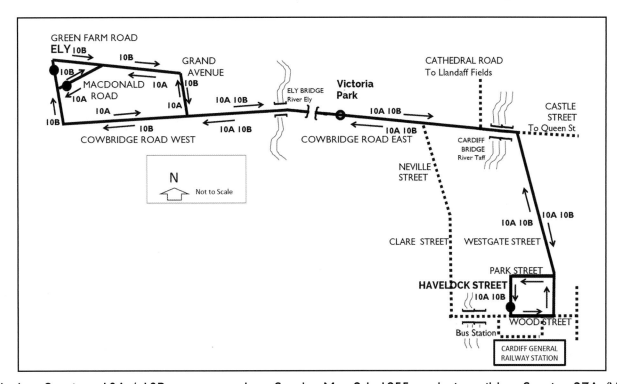

Trolleybus Services 10A / 10B commenced on Sunday May 8th 1955, replacing oil-bus Service 27A (Wood St. – Ely). Due to an industrial dispute, the last day of trolleybus operation on these services was December 3rd 1969, the services being replaced the following day by oil-buses. Commencing Sunday January 11th 1970, the two Services officially changed over to oil-bus operation, the 10A and 10B becoming Services 14 and 15 respectively.

BUT /East Lancs 285 is on its way from Roath Depot to Havelock Street to take-up duties on the Ely services. It is seen using the short section of wiring (used only by trolleybuses entering service) connecting Castle Street with Westgate Street in March 1965.
Colin Hewlett

Further along Westgate Street, BUT/East Lancs 277 is turning right into Park Street during the summer of 1962. Due to the many underground cables from the nearby telephone exchange, and the difficulties in finding suitable sites to erect traction posts, the overhead was suspended from rosettes attached to the Central Post Office building (to the left).

D.A.Thompson

The city centre terminal point for Services 10A/B was in Havelock Street (not Wood Street as shown on destination blinds), where BUT/East Lancs 216 is waiting to depart on its next journey to Ely in August 1963. In the background, a Cardiff Corporation 1949 Crossley motorbus has just left the Central Bus Station and is turning into Wood Street.

M.Gylee

Looking in the opposite direction to the previous photograph, newly repainted BUT/East Lancs 287 waits at the Havelock Street treminus in September 1965 for its next departure to Ely. The building in the background is the GPO mail sorting office (now closed). *Colin Hewlett*

BUT/East Lancs 275 has just turned out of Westgate Street into Castle Street on its way to Ely in July 1968. The shape of the trailing frog leaves much to be desired, and is the result of a badly fitting extruded runner. *John White*

BUT/East Lancs 220 is working an inbound 10B, and has just passed through the junction of Cowbridge Road East with Cathedral Road in March 1969. When the 10A/B Services commenced in 1955, there was just one set of traffic lights (at Cathedral Road junction) between Havelock Street and Green Farm Road. Today, there are thirty-five sets.   *Author*

BUT/Bruce Coachworks 270 is outbound on a 10A duty and passing through St. David's junction in Cowbridge Road East on 29th April 1966. Removal of the overhead junction (previously used by Services 5A/B) is in progress and the crossover 270 has just passed through will be cut-down in the early hours of the following day.   *John White*

BUT/East Lancs 275 on an inward 10B journey, is loading passengers at the junction of Cowbridge Road East with Wyndham Crescent, Canton, on 27th April 1968. The properties on the left (including the erstwhile Donald Knight drapery store) have long since been demolished and replaced by offices and a supermarket.

John White

BUT/East Lancs 220 travels along Cowbridge Road East, Canton, on its way to Ely in June 1968. In the background (left) is the junction with Llandaff Road and on the corner is the Corporation Hotel (now closed). *Colin Hewlett*

Pausing to pick up a passenger in Cowbridge Road East, Canton, is BUT/ East Lancs 220 on 15th February 1968. In the background (left) is Beda Road, which formed part of a little used short working facility until its removal in June 1965. Evidence of the former trailing frog at this location can be seen by the splicing ears immediately behind the trolley heads of 220. *John White*

When this view was taken, Canton was one of Cardiff's busiest suburban shopping areas, with many people using the 10A/B trolleybuses to travel in from Ely to do their shopping. BUT/East Lancs 276 is seen passing the F.W. Woolworth's store in Cowbridge Road East on April 19th 1969. *John White*

BUT/East Lancs 218 has come to grief after passing through a power feeder in Cowbridge Road West, a short distance after leaving Victoria Park on July 15th 1968. Luckily it is a Sunday morning, and road traffic is light as the driver and conductor try to re-connect the booms with the wires. *John White*

BUT/East Lancs 278 working inbound on the 10B Service is viewed overtaking BUT/Bruce Coachworks 273 at the Victoria Park Terminus of Service 8 on 15th February 1968. In tramway days, Victoria Park was a major interchange point where tram services terminated, and connected with motorbus services serving the vast Ely Council Housing Estate. *John White*

BUT/East Lancs 222 is negotiating Ely Bridge (Cowbridge Road West) roundabout working an inbound 10A Service on 11th September 1966. This vehicle retained many of its original bodywork features right up until final withdrawal from service (just one month later). This extremely busy junction is now controlled by a mini roundabout. *John White*

BUT/East Lancs 287 regains speed after passing beneath the railway bridge carrying the former Taff Vale Railway Penarth Branch (the present-day 'City-Line') over Cowbridge Road West on 31st August 1968. Hancock's Beer was brewed locally by William Hancock & Co. Ltd. until the company was acquired by Bass Charrington in 1968 and renamed Welsh Brewers.

John White

BUT/East Lancs 285 working a 10B Service to Ely has just passed the junction of Cowbridge Road West and Grand Avenue in February 1967. The 10A and 10B Services diverged at this point to form two loops, the 10B continuing along Cowbridge Road West to form the outer loop, whilst the 10A turned right into Grand Avenue to form the inner loop. The wiring entering Grand Avenue can just be seen to the far left in this view.

John White

Further along Cowbridge Road West, BUT/East Lancs 275 is outbound on the 10B and has just passed the Dusty Forge Inn on 30th March 1968. Work commenced on building the Ely Council Estate in the early 1920's to provide 'homes fit for heroes' and to rehouse residents from Cardiff's inner-city slums.

John White

An overhead breakdown (the negative trolley wire has come adrift from the ear) in Cowbridge Road West (A48 trunk road), where BUT/East Lancs 283 is carrying out a battery manoeuvre to pass the Bedford tower wagon on 25th April 1968. The conductor is carrying the bamboo pole ready to place the booms back on the wires.

John White

BUT/East Lancs 275 is turning from Cowbridge Road West into Green Farm Road on 29th June 1967. The view shows the close proximity of the rear platform to the road surface at this point, and the reason why the container for the bamboo pole was raised into the rear panel. Passing in the opposite direction is BUT/East Lancs 281.   *M.J. Russell*

One-in-three journeys on the 10B Service left the main route at the junction of Green Farm Road with MacDonald Road and continued to Green Farm Road terminus using a single-line loop. BUT/East Lancs 227 has taken the outer set of wires at the frog to reach the MacDonald Road terminal point in December 1968. The inner set of wires lead to the Green Farm Road terminus.

John White

BUT/East Lancs 227 has arrived at the MacDonald Road terminus of Service 10A in June 1968. In the background is BUT/ East Lancs 275 on the 10B Service. To ease road congestion when both a 10A and 10B trolleybuses were waiting at the terminal, a layby was constructed for use by 10B trolleybuses (as shown in this view).   *R.F. Mack Courtesy NTA 1963*

BUT/East Lancs 227 is viewed at the Green Farm Road 10B terminus (adjacent to the Western Cemetery) on November 11th 1969. The loop was about three quarters of a mile long, and only wired in one direction. Service 10B had in effect two termini points at Ely (Green Farm Road and MacDonald Road).   *Author's Collection*

A tour of the trolleybus system using Bournemouth open-top trolleybus 202 was held on Sunday October 5th 1969. In this view, the booms on BUT/East Lancs 220 have been lowered to allow 202 to pass on the single-line wiring in Green Farm Road. The extremely rundown condition of the remaining trolleybuses during the final days of the system, is clearly shown with the dented panels, peeling paintwork and lack of rear route number blind on 220. *John White*

BUT/East Lancs 227 on Service 10B in June 1967, is seen leaving MacDonald Road and cutting across the central reservation in Grand Avenue, to join the wiring entering from the Green Farm Road loop. *M.J. Russell*

BUT/East Lancs 280 is captured in glorious sunshine in Grand Avenue working towards the MacDonald Road terminus on route 10A on 6th October 1968. When the Ely housing estate was being built, provision for tramway operation was made in Grand Avenue with a central reservation to accommodate sleeper track. However, the tramway was never extended to Ely.

John White

The snow is beginning to melt as BUT/East Lancs 284 passes Ely Gospel Hall in Grand Avenue whilst working a 10A Service to Ely on 21st February 1967. The Ely Council Housing Estate was at one-time the largest such estate in Europe. On Weekdays (1955 Timetable) the first trolleybus to Ely departed Roath Depot at 4:05am, which was the earliest departure on the system (return from Ely was at 4:43am). A new reduced depth destination blind, requiring masking to be applied to prevent overlapping of the route details, has been fitted to 284.

John White

Diversions on Rugby International Days

On Rugby International Saturdays, the 10A/B Services were affected by spectators using Westgate Street to access the venue where the games were played. Diversions were brought into use on these days, and making a right-hand turn (normally prohibited) from Castle Street into High Street is BUT/East Lancs 276 on Saturday 15th April 1967.

John White

BUT/East Lancs 281 has travelled from Wood Street, and is turning from Tudor Road into Clare Street whilst working a diverted 10B Service to Ely in November 1963. It will regain the normal route to Ely at the junction of Neville Street with Cowbridge Road. After a weight restriction was imposed on Wood Street Bridge in December 1965, this diversionary route was no longer available for use by trolleybuses on international days.

John White

BUT'S 223, 273 and 255 have been diverted to travel inward via Castle Street, High Street and St. Mary Street to a temporary terminal point in Wood Street on 3rd December 1966 (Wales vs Australia). After loading, their outward route will be via the General Station turning loop, St. Mary Street, High Street and Castle Street to regain the normal route at the junction of Castle Street and Westgate Street.
John White

By the time this photograph was taken (8th March 1969), there was no alternative diversion route available for the 10A/B Services to use on International Rugby Saturdays. As a result, trolleybuses operated as normal through Westgate Street in both directions. BUT/East Lancs 227, on an inward 10A Service makes its way cautiously through the crowds heading for the match.
John White

Westgate Street One-Way Scheme 1967

A new one-way traffic scheme came into effect on 26th November 1967 (which reversed the direction of travel and required realignment to the overhead) in Park Street, Wood Street, Havelock Street and Westgate Street. BUT/Bruce Coachworks 258 is seen passing the overhead crew erecting a new bracket arm in Westgate Street on 23rd October 1967.
John White

New wiring, together with a hand-operated frog were installed in Westgate Street, enabling trolleybuses to travel to the terminus in Havelock Street or to Roath Depot directly via St. Mary Street. BUT /East Lancs 276 is about to pass through the frog on its way to Havelock Street in June 1968.
Colin Hewlett

This short section of Westgate Street was previously a two-way highway, becoming one-way in a southerly direction as part of the new traffic scheme. BUT/East Lancs 218 is approaching the junction with Wood Street on July 6th 1968, where it will turn right, then right again into Havelock Street.
Author

The direction of traffic along Havelock Street was also reversed, and the terminal point for Services 10A/B relocated from the east to the west side, where BUT/East Lancs 281 is seen resting between duties on 17th May 1969. *David Christie*

After leaving the terminal point in Havelock Street, BUT/East Lancs 283 rounds the corner into Park Street and will shortly turn left into Westgate Street on 31st August 1968.   *John White*

Having completed duties on the 10A/B services, BUT/East Lancs 276 is returning to Roath Depot displaying former route No. 8, as it leaves Westgate Street heading left towards St. Mary Street on 31st August 1968.   *John White*

During reconstruction in Cowbridge Road West of the old bridge over the River Ely in 1969, three Bailey Bridges were temporarily built alongside the old bridge and new overhead wiring erected to allow trolleybuses to use two of them. This view shows overhead linesmen attaching a bracket arm to a newly planted traction pole on 2nd June 1969. *Colin Hewlett*

An unidentified west bound trolleybus using one of the Bailey Bridges over the River Ely (which can be seen in the foreground) on 1st July 1969.

Colin Hewlett

Until the Bailey bridges were fully constructed and wired for trolleybuses to use, inward trolleybuses continued to use the old bridge over the River Ely. This rear view of BUT/East Lancs 279 taken in August 1969, shows the 'Trolleybus Only' signs warning other traffic not to use the inside lane of the old bridge.   *John White*

The bracket arms (on the left) are ready for the inbound overhead wires to be attached (this work was carried out on 14th July 1969). When all three bridges were completed, the middle bridge was restricted to the peak-hour direction of travel. BUT/East Lancs 285 is heading west on 1st July 1969, whilst Western Welsh Leyland Atlantean 313 is using the middle Bailey Bridge.   *John White*

SERVICE 16
MONUMENT - PIER HEAR (DOCKS)

via Mill Lane - Monument – Bute Street – Pier Head (Docks)

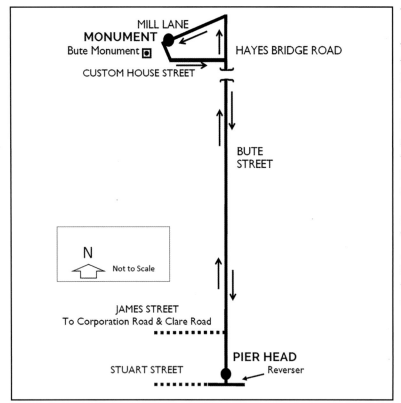

Trolleybus Service 16 commenced Sunday 17th August 1947, replacing tram route No. 16. Trams had been withdrawn from the route on 27th April 1946 and the service had been temporarily operated by motor buses from that date. The length of the route was 1.24 miles The route was renumbered 14 on 1st July 1962.

Route 16 connected the city centre with the Docks area via Bute Street. In the early 20th century, this thoroughfare was described as rough, and an area regarded by chapel-goers as awash with whisky and streaming with scarlet women.

First departure from the Monument (1955 Timetable) Weekdays and Saturdays was 5:12-am, with a 3/4/5-minute frequency thereafter until 11:00-pm. Sundays every 20 minutes from 6:05-am until midday, thereafter every 10 minutes until 10:45-pm. The last day of trolleybus operation was Saturday 11th January 1964; replaced by extending oil-bus Service No. 2 (St. Mary Street – Pengam) to operate Pier Head – Pengam.

English Electric 231 was one of seven similar trolleybuses purchased second-hand from Pontypridd UDC in 1947 as a stop-gap measure due to a delay in delivery of new trolleybuses (all were withdrawn from service by late 1950). It is seen waiting at the Monument terminus (located at that time on the bridge crossing the Glamorganshire Canal) for its next trip to the Pier Head, circa 1949.

Author's Collection

Brush car No. 3 (built in 1925) is about to turn from Mill Lane into St. Mary Street on 14th April 1939. On the corner is the Terminus Hotel with its prominent adverts for Ely Ales & Stout. The building remains to this day but in the form of a night club. The Glamorganshire Canal is just visible on the extreme right.

H.B. Priestley, courtesy National Tramway Museum

After the completion of roadworks and the filling-in of the Glamorganshire Canal, the Monument terminal point for Service 16 was relocated to Mill Lane during 1950/1. BUT/East Lancs 239 is viewed at the Mill Lane terminus in July 1961. AEC Regent III/Bruce Coachworks 17 is behind, working Service 39 to Manor Way. *D.A.Thompson*

BUT/East Lancs 243 is leaving Mill Lane and about to turn into Custom House Street on its way to the Pier Head on 11th January 1964 (the last day of single-deck trolleybus operation on route 14). This view also clearly shows the special 20ft bow-string bracket arms (instead of the maximum regulation length of 16ft.) in use at this location. *John White*

BUT/East Lancs 242 is turning out of Custom House Street and entering Bute Street on its way to the Docks in July 1961. On its return from the Pier Head, 242 will travel straight across this junction into Hayes Bridge Road in order to access Mill Lane. The Golden Cross public house in the background (with its distinctive ceramic tiling) has survived and is now Grade II Listed. *D.A.Thompson*

The restrictive height (15ft. 0in.) of the bridge at the northern end of Bute Street, prohibited the operation of double-deck trolleybuses on this route. BUT/East Lancs 241 is approaching the junction of Bute Street with John Street, on the way to the Pier Head in July 1961. *D.A.Thompson*

BUT/East Lancs 241 passes through the junction of Bute Street with James Street, and is now only a short distance away from the Pier Head in March 1963. This area was home to many businesses associated with the Docks, such as ship's chandlers, brokers, coal exporters and bunkering agents. In the distance (to the left of 241 in this view), is Bute Road Railway Station. *M. Gylee*

After entering Stuart Street, BUT/East Lancs 242 is slowly reversing across the end of Bute Street into Bute Crescent in August 1963. The conductor is standing at the rear to supervise this procedure. The former Cardiff Railway Headquarters (with its imposing clock tower) forms the backdrop. *C. Carter*

BUT/East Lancs 241 has arrived at the Pier Head terminus, located at the southern end of Bute Street, in July 1961. In readiness for the return trip to The Monument, 241 will turn by means of a triangular reverser, and for the first part of this procedure it will now turn right into Stuart Street.
D.A.Thompson

After reversing into Bute Crescent, English Electric 236 will now pull forward to proceed to the loading point in Bute Street on January 25th 1948. The Cardiff Bay Development has in recent years completely transformed this once unique area of Cardiff docklands, and sadly nothing remains of this scene today.

Author

Seen at the same location as the previous picture, this June 1963 view shows BUT/East Lancs 239 about to pull forward into Bute Street. The building in the background was demolished in the early 1970's, and replaced by Welsh Industrial and Maritime Museum. The museum closed in 1998 as part of the Cardiff Bay Development.

M. Gylee

The proximity of the sea at the Pier Head reverser is evident in this view of BUT/East Lancs 238 leaving the reversing triangle on the final operating day of route 14 (Saturday 11th January 1964). The semaphore signals (in the background) directed incoming pleasure boats to their appointed berths at the floating pontoons.   *John White*

A view of Bute Street from the Pier Head looking north. BUT/East Lancs 239 will shortly pull into the loading point (next to the first visible bracket arm) before commencing another journey to the Monument.   *M. Gylee*

BUT/East Lancs 240 is on a return trip to the Monument from the Pier Head, and will go straight across this junction at the top of Bute Street into Hayes Bridge Road, and then turn left into Mill Lane. A hand-frog (just beyond the feeder) allowed trolleybuses to turn left into Custom House Street to bypass Mill Lane on Depot journeys. *Author's Collection*

BUT/East Lancs 241 is turning from Hayes Bridge Road into Mill Lane in August 1963. Considerable redevelopment has since taken place in this area, and nothing remains of this scene today. *Author's Collection*

BUT/East Lancs 243 is waiting at the Monument terminus of Service 16 in Mill Lane before its next departure for the Pier Head in July 1961. 243 was the last three-axle single-deck trolleybus to be built in Great Britain. *D.A.Thompson*

The wiring in Custom House Street (east to west) saw little use other than for trolleybuses returning to Roath Depot. BUT/East Lancs 238 is shown using this short section of wiring in December 1963. *John White*

QUEEN STREET ONE-WAY SYSTEM 1965

Queen Street became one-way, east to west from October 31st 1965. New overhead wire was erected between Duke Street and Dumfries Place to enable eastbound trolleybuses to comply with the new road layout. This view shows work being undertaken in Duke Street to install new wiring in Kingsway and the Civic Centre on a Sunday morning in September 1965.

CTPG

A view taken after commencement of the new one-way scheme, showing BUT/East Lancs 229 about to turn into Kingsway from Duke Street working eastbound on Service 4. A short section of the old wiring was retained at this point for power supply purposes.

R.F. Mack courtesy NTA 1963

BUT/East Lancs (Bridlington) 249 is climbing the short gradient in Kingsway on 30th March 1968. The quadrangular tower of St. John The Baptist Church is seen in the background, whilst the premises of E.R. Force (a former coach proprietor) is visible on the left.

John White

This view shows BUT/Bruce Coachworks 255 in Cathays Park Road, working a Service 4 to Roath Park on April 24th 1966. The City Hall and Law Courts feature prominently in the background. Following a collision with a tree in Newport Road on February 2nd 1964, the front dome area on 255 was extensively rebuilt and rubber mounted windows fitted.

John White

A Winter Wonderland scene in Cardiff Civic Centre, showing BUT/East Lancs 216 as it travels eastwards to Roath Park following an overnight snowfall on 9th December 1967. Its roof is covered in snow, probably as a result of being parked overnight in the open at Roath Depot. Cardiff City Hall (opened in 1906) forms a perfect backdrop. *John White*

BUT/East Lancs 223 has just entered Dumfries Place after leaving Cathays Park Road on 19th June 1966. It is about to pass through a power feeder, for which a new cable was laid from a section box in Queen Street. *Peter Mitchell*

The new one-way system ended at the junction of Dumfries Place and Queen Street, where BUT/East Lancs 215 is seen working eastwards on Service 8 in July 1967. In the background is the former Alexandra Hotel (since demolished and replaced by a shopping centre). Queen Street is in the background. *CTPG*

JOURNEY'S END

BUT/Bruce Coachworks 262 was purchased by a group of Cardiff trolleybus enthusiasts in November 1968 and subsequently operated several tours over the Cardiff system before it closed. It is seen here on a test run in Green Farm Road on 17th May 1969, prior to operating a tour the following day.
David Christie

A view of 262 at the junction of Cowbridge Road West and Grand Avenue, whilst operating a tour of the Cardiff system on Sunday 18th May 1969.
David Christie

On the final day of trolleybus operation (Sunday 11th January 1970), 262 is about to make the normally prohibited right turn from Castle Street into High Street. Special dispensation was obtained from the Police Authority for this to occur.

David Christie

262 arrives at Roath Depot for the final time on Sunday 11th January 1970. It was driven through the Depot to the rear parking area, where the booms were kept on the wires until the power supply was switched off twenty minutes or so after this view was taken.

David Christie

The overhead crew are working in Dumfries Place removing a redundant traction post, shown being manoeuvred onto the Bristol K6A poling wagon, in October 1970.

Author

An acetylene torch is being used to cut-off the jagged remnants of a traction pole base at Dumfries Place in October 1970. The hole would subsequently be filled with crushed bricks (seen on the extreme right).

Author

Removal of overhead in Queen Street during March 1970. Caerphilly UDC Leyland PD3 No. 32 passes between the two tower wagons. Queen Street is now a pedestrianised area. *John White*

After being withdrawn from service, many Cardiff trolleybuses ended their days in Bill Way's scrapyard, situated on the edge of the Bute East Dock. This view shows part of the yard on 2nd July 1977. In the background, a smoky haze rises from the chimneys of the East Moors Steelworks (closed in 1978). *R. Helliar-Symons*

An unusual view of the booms of BUT/Bruce 254, as it awaits the scrapman's torch in Bill Way's scrapyard on 2nd July 1977. Has it crossed its booms in the hope of being spared? *R. Helliar-Symons*

Four Cardiff trolleybuses (203, 215, 243 and 262) are fortunately preserved. 203 resides at the Sandtoft Trolleybus Museum and is the only Cardiff trolleybus currently restored to full working condition. It is seen in May 2010, after undergoing a major refurbishment by The British Trolleybus Society (including being repainted in the early post-war 'streamlined' livery. *Author's Collection*

ILLUMINATED VEHICLES

AEC/Northern Counties 206 is seen in Wood Street on Service 6 in December 1962. The last of the AEC trolleybuses were withdrawn in June 1965.

Tony Belton

Following the withdrawal of the AEC trolleybuses, the tradition of illuminated trolleybuses during the Christmas period was retained by using BUT trolleybuses. To keep costs to a minimum, the illuminated discs used in previous years on the AEC vehicles were attached to the front of the BUT trolleybuses involved. This view shows 228 at the Pier Head in December 1965.

Colin Hewlett

Additional funding for the illuminations in 1966, saw the use of coloured bulbs attached to the perimeter of a wooden frame mounted over the front destination box. BUT/East Lancs 227 is seen at Gabalfa on December 16th 1967.

Robin Helliar-Symons

BUT/East Lancs 218 is seen in Castle Street on its way to Ely on Service 10A in December 1968. Generally, the illuminations were switched off on the last day of December.

John White

Cardiff gained quite a reputation with trolleybus enthusiasts for the operation of illuminated trolleybuses during the Christmas period. In this December 1968 view, BUT/East Lancs 218 is in Havelock Street on a 10A working.

M. J. Russell

In this December 1968 view, passengers are boarding BUT/Bruce 255 at the 10A terminus in Havelock Street. Note the plate (hung beneath the near-side windscreen) giving destination details, including 'GWR STATION' which was anachronism even when 255 was new in 1949, the Great Western Railway being nationalised in 1948. *M. J. Russell*

TROLLEYBUS FLEET LIST
CARDIFF CORPORATION TRANSPORT

FLEET No.	REGISTRATION No.	CHASSIS	BODY	NEW
201-210	CKG 191-200	AEC	Northern Counties H38/32R	1942-3
211-220	DBO 471-480	BUT	East Lancashire H38/29D	1948
221-230	DUH 716-725	BUT	East Lancashire H38/29D	1948
231	TG 379	E/E	English Electric B32C	1931
232	TG 281	E/E	English Electric B32C	1931
233	TG 283	E/E	English Electric B32C	1931
234	TG 285	E/E	English Electric B32C	1931
235	TG 287	E/E	English Electric B32C	1931
236	TG 289	E/E	English Electric B32C	1931
237	TG 291	E/E	English Electric B32C	1931
238-242	EBO 891-895	BUT	East Lancashire B38D	1949
243	KBO 961	BUT	East Lancashire B40R	1955
245/6/7/9/50	EBO 902/3/4/6/7	BUT	East Lancashire H38/29D	1950
248/51-64	EBO 905/8-921	BUT	Bruce Coachworks H38/29D	1949/50
265-274	FBO 85-94	BUT	Bruce Coachworks H38/29D	1950
275-287	KBO 948-960	BUT	East Lancashire H38/29D	1955

Notes:

201-210 AEC 664T Chassis fitted with English Electric control equipment.

211-230, 238-242, 243, 245-287 BUT 9641T Chassis fitted with GEC control equipment.

245/6/7/9/50 fitted with East Lancashire (Bridlington) bodywork.

236-237 EE-SD6WTB Chassis fitted with English Electric control equipment. Vehicles purchased from Pontypridd Urban District Council in 1946.

Bruce Coachworks was a local coach building firm in business between 1945-1952.

BUT/East Lancs 218 is on learner duties and has just crossed Wood Street from Central Square into Havelock Street on May 5th 1968. The shelters for the 10A/B terminus can be seen just ahead of 218. This area has changed considerably in recent times, and today only the building on the right survives. *John White*

DEPOTS

Clare Road Depot

Clare Road Depot opened in March 1902. Built as a nine-track dead-ended building, it was enlarged in 1925 in anticipation of the tramway system being extended to the newly built Ely council housing estate. BUT/East Lancs 230 is shown outside the Depot in 1949. *Author's Collection*

Clare Road Depot was converted for trolleybus use in 1945/6. Space was extremely limited within the building, and trolleybuses would often be parked alongside the Depot in Pendyris Street. This view shows BUT/East Lancs 226 leaving the Depot to enter service. The Depot was closed as an economy measure in October 1953. *Author's Collection*

AEC/Northern Counties 201 is parked alongside other AEC trolleybuses in the Depot yard on 9th September 1962. During the First World War, part of the Depot was converted into a munitions factory, manufacturing shell cases for the war effort. The cost of the machinery necessary for the fabrication of the cases was borne personally by the Tramways General Manager (Arthur Ellis).

John White

A line-up of withdrawn single-deck trolleybuses parked at the rear of the Depot on 22nd February 1964. BUT/East Lancs 239 is the leading vehicle.

David Pearson

There was very little parking space available within the depot building, and most of the trolleybus fleet was parked in the adjoining large open-air yard. The building in the background is Roath Power Station, opened in 1902 to supply power to the new tram system. It closed in 1969. *Author's Collection*

Trolleybus 207 heads a line-up of AECs in Roath Depot on 7th September 1965. After the closure of the trolleybus system in 1970, Roath Depot remained opened for the operation of oil-buses until April 1980; and was then retained as a repair and overhaul facility until 1986. A supermarket now occupies the site. *Peter Mitchell*

BUT/East Lancs 227 is seen parked alongside Alexander bodied AEC Swift 509 in April 1969. By this time there were only about 15 trolleybuses left in service, and only two 'roads' were allocated for their parking. *Author*

On the west side of the Depot a lane (complete with tram track and granite-setts), allowed trolleybuses to access the parking area at the rear of the building without traveling through the Depot itself. AEC/Northern Counties 210 is shown using this facility on 15th November 1962. *Tony Belton*

Seen leaving Roath Depot to take up duties in the evening peak period, AEC/Northern Counties 207, closely followed by similar vehicle 201, negotiate crossing the busy main A48 trunk road in August 1962. In the background, roadworks to alter the junction are in progress, whilst the trolleybus wiring to Pengam is also visible. *John White*

The same location and manoeuvre as in the previous photograph, but here being undertaken by BUT/East Lancs 213 and 218 in July 1966. Note that the road junction is now under the control of traffic lights, giving trolleybus drivers a much better opportunity to leave the depot. *Colin Hewlett*

MAPS

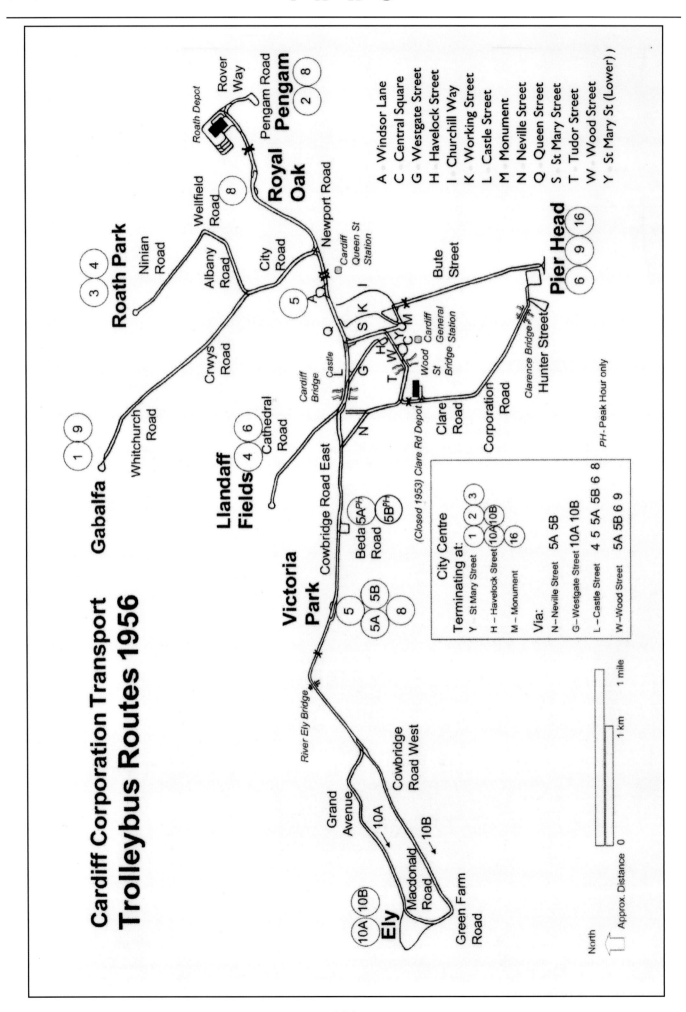

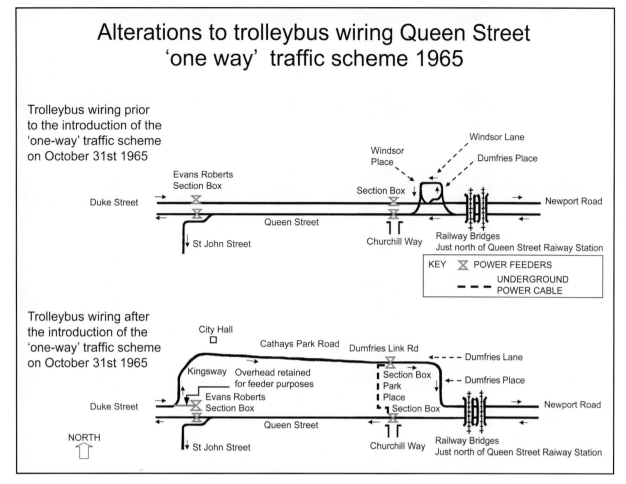

Alterations to trolleybus wiring Queen Street
'one way' traffic scheme 1965

Trolleybus wiring prior
to the introduction of the
'one-way' traffic scheme
on October 31st 1965

Windsor Lane

Windsor Place

Dumfries Place

Evans Roberts
Section Box

Section Box

Duke Street

Newport Road

Queen Street

St John Street

Churchill Way

Railway Bridges
Just north of Queen Street Raiway Station

KEY   POWER FEEDERS

UNDERGROUND
POWER CABLE

Trolleybus wiring after
the introduction of the
'one-way' traffic scheme
on October 31st 1965

City Hall

Cathays Park Road

Dumfries Link Rd

Dumfries Lane

Kingsway   Overhead retained
for feeder purposes

Section Box

Dumfries Place

Park
Place

Evans Roberts
Section Box

Duke Street

Section Box

Newport Road

Queen Street

NORTH

St John Street

Churchill Way

Railway Bridges
Just north of Queen Street Raiway Station

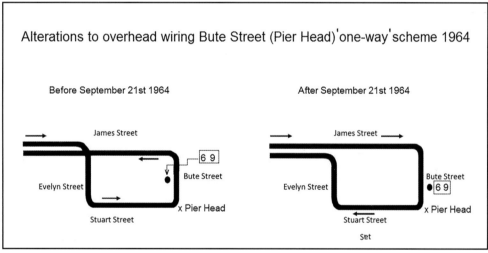

Alterations to overhead wiring Bute Street (Pier Head)'one-way'scheme 1964

Before September 21st 1964

After September 21st 1964

James Street

James Street

6 9

Evelyn Street

Bute Street

Evelyn Street

Bute Street

6 9

Stuart Street

x Pier Head

Stuart Street

x Pier Head

Set

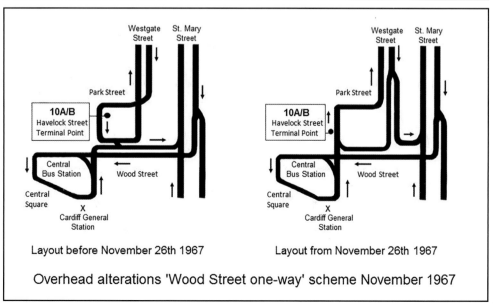

Westgate
Street

St. Mary
Street

Westgate
Street

St. Mary
Street

Park Street

Park Street

10A/B
Havelock Street
Terminal Point

10A/B
Havelock Street
Terminal Point

Central
Bus Station

Wood Street

Central
Bus Station

Wood Street

Central
Square

X
Cardiff General
Station

Central
Square

X
Cardiff General
Station

Layout before November 26th 1967

Layout from November 26th 1967

Overhead alterations 'Wood Street one-way' scheme November 1967

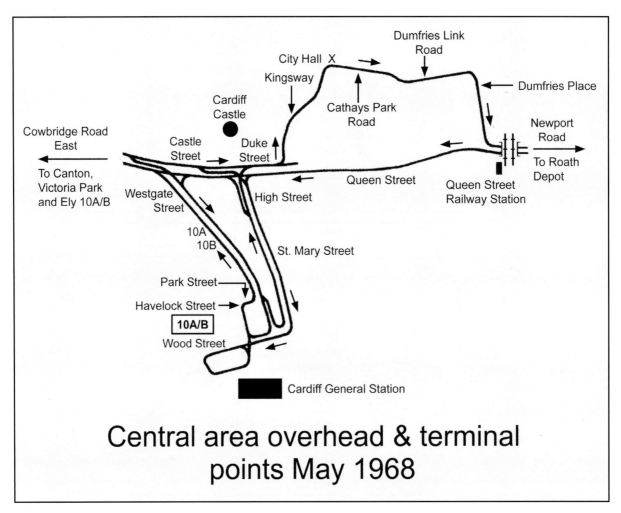

Central area overhead & terminal points May 1968

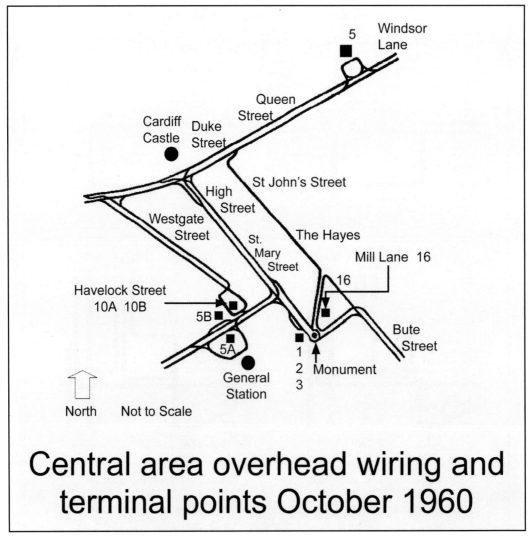

Central area overhead wiring and terminal points October 1960